D1235007

NEPAL

Modernity, Multiculturalism and Marginalisation

Sanjaya Serchan

Published by
Senfdin
Kathmandu

ISBN: 978-9937-2-2085-9

Price NRs 200
US $ 5

Computer Type & Design
Rajesh Tandukar
Phone: 4992499, 9841345999

Acknowledgements

As the first decade of the twenty-first century draws to a close, the world seems to be confronted with new issues and problems. The euphoria of the early 1990s following the end of the Cold War or the exuberance a decade later at the beginning of a new century and a new millennium appear today as distant memories. On an even longer time-scale, one could point to the issues and problems that we face today as challenging the West and the modernity it had engendered of the last couple of centuries.

This book is an attempt to delve into some of the issues and problems confronting us today, namely the assertiveness of non-Western societies vis-à-vis the "project of modernity." The book, while analysing the current situation, focuses primarily on the Nepalese context. Nonetheless, attempt has been made to also look at the larger context, given that, in today's interconnected world, the "national" and the "global" are inextricably intertwined. As usual, while writing this book, I have gained considerably from the inputs and insights from friends and colleagues. Dev Raj Dahal and Mahendra Lawoti read earlier drafts of the book and provided perceptive comments and suggestions. I thank them both while at the same time stating that they are in no way responsible for the errors, of interpretation and otherwise, that remain in the book.

The publication of this book was partially funded by the National Foundation for Development of Indigenous Nationalities (NFDIN). I would like to thank NFDIN and its Vice-Chairperson Jitpal Kirat for assisting in the book's publication.

Contents

1

Introduction

The events of September 11, 2001 are said to have brought to an end the post-cold war world order. The 9/11 attacks on the United States, the lone and unrivalled superpower, have appeared as an event marking the end of an era. The fall of the Berlin Wall in 1989 and the collapse of communist regimes in the Soviet Union and in Eastern Europe had led to a resurgence of democracy, thus raising hopes of the triumph of liberal democracy all over the world. The ending of the decades-long cold war between two bitterly divided ideological camps had, not unsurprisingly, raised expectations of a new world order and of the demise of autocratic and totalitarian systems around the world and their replacement by Western-style democracies. And a democratic resurgence did indeed sweep the world, leading to the collapse of dictators and dictatorial regimes in many countries. The impact of the events beyond was felt also in Nepal, where a Popular Movement ended the three-decade long partyless Panchayat system in 1990 and restored multiparty democracy in the country.

The tearing down of the Berlin Wall, the toppling of statues of communist leaders in communist countries by masses of ecstatic crowds, images of which were beamed via television to living rooms around the world, provided the impetus to democratic movements in numerous countries. In this context, the new order post-1989 supposedly heralded the victory of Western liberal democratic ideology. It was perhaps not entirely surprising in these circumstances the note of triumphalism among some Western intellectuals, as an ascendant West saw the rest of the world being recreated in its own image. Countries around the world, many of them considered undeveloped, not fully democratic, backward and illiberal societies, were to follow the path taken by the industrialised democracies of the West during their course of development over the years. Thus, the West and the modernity it had engendered was to emerge victorious and encompass the entire world.

Indeed, as long entrenched autocratic regimes—one-party, partyless, military, etc.—fell, the forward march of democracy appeared inevitable. Of course, there was always the possibility that with the spread of democracy among the masses all kinds of local assertiveness would come to the fore. Adult franchise not only brought an Aung San Suu Kyi, but would also bring the Islamic Salvation Front in Algeria, or the Hamas in Palestine. In Nepal, the political change of 1990 had been spearheaded by political parties with modernist inclinations, viz. the 'social democratic' Nepali Congress and the United Left Front made up of seven communist parties. These parties were instrumental in drafting a new constitution following 1990. The constitution, however, continued with the appellation of the Hindu state of the previous partyless Panchayat regime, along with disregarding to a large extent the voices related to language, culture, etc. raised by the diverse groups of the Nepalese society. The new constitution, thus, gave continuity to the norms and values of the dominant sociocultural groups of the Nepalese society, the Khas-Nepali speaking hill Hindu "high" caste groups.

The Nepalese state during its very making itself subverted and marginalised groups like the indigenous nationalities, *dalit, Madhesi,* mother tongue speakers, non-Hindus, women and people of the remote regions of the country. The assimilationistic project of the nation-state negated the multicultural reality of the Nepalese society. The gradual consolidation of the Nepalese state led to the imposition by the dominant groups of their language, culture, religion and way of life all over Nepal as the "national" language, culture, religion and way of life. The modern phenomenon of the nation-state, thus, not only strengthened the traditional values of the dominant groups in the Nepalese society but also led to their diffusion throughout the society. This happened as the way of life of the dominant groups came to be seen as the way of life of a single, universal and unified and homogenous 'Nepali people/nation.'

Nevertheless, the opening up of the political space following the democratic change of 1990 has meant that the voices at the margins are increasingly coming to the forefront. In this context, the monolithic nationalism traditionally espoused by the Nepalese state has come under attack from diverse sections of the Nepalese society. During the drafting of the new constitution after 1990, a major demand of non-Hindus and groups like the indigenous nationalities had been for a secular state. The constitution writing process had seen the aspirations of the sociocultural groups of the Nepalese society. The majority of suggestions submitted by various organisations and peoples to the Constitution Recommendation Commission, the body responsible for drafting the constitution, had been related to language, culture, religion, etc. These suggestions included, along with the demand for a secular state, the use of the various languages in government bodies to calls for federalism and autonomy. All these issues, and related ones that have come to accumulate along the way, have only increased in intensity over the years, as long oppressed and marginalised groups seek for their place in the post-1990 democratic Nepalese polity.

One cannot of course view the challenges the Nepalese state is facing today in isolation. They are part of the wider trends across the world. If we look back at the twentieth century, we can see the anti-colonial struggles and the struggle for nationhood in developing countries around the world. The mid-twentieth century had particularly been the period of "nationalist" struggles, with de-colonisation being the norm. Countries in Asia and Africa threw off their imperial yoke and attempted to build a nation out of what was primarily a diverse population living within their territories. The nation building project in developing countries, generally similar to that in developed countries which it sought to emulate, was assimilationistic in nature, thus negating the multicultural reality of the societies they inhabited. In Nepal, the project of nation building reached its apogee during the King-led Panchayat system, with its slogan of 'our king, our country: one language, one dress.'

Today, of course, at the turn of the twenty-first century, another kind of wind is blowing across the world, as groups and peoples seek to identify with their own particular ties of cultures, languages, religions, etc. Thus, the challenges facing the Nepalese state can be seen as part of a deeper malaise throughout the world. They are symptomatic of the challenge posed to an ascendant West of the last couple of centuries, along with the modernity it had engendered. They signify an attack on the 'Enlightenment project' and the hopes for human well-being it had given rise to. All this is borne out for instance by the numerous "posts" that have appeared in the intellectual discourse of our times. Besides postmodern, there is post-capitalist, post-industrial, post-liberal, post-identity, post-racial, post-historical, post-national, post-feminist and even post-humanity.

We live in times marked by 'the end of ideology,' where all "isms" are said to have been turned into "wasms." The upheavals around the world, including that in Nepal, seem to suggest a shift in the way we perceive things. By challenging established viewpoints, they appear to point to a fundamental rethink in our long held worldviews and perspectives. What are the causes behind these upheavals? What are their implications? What will be their consequences? I have attempted here to delve into these questions. This book attempts to look into the current debates raging related to ethnicity, culture, language, religion, etc.

Although I have in this book analysed the ongoing situation with particular focus on the Nepalese society, I also nevertheless attempt to look into the wider trends at the global level. This appears inevitable given the interconnectedness of the events within the country and beyond. And when focusing on the Nepalese society, I focus in particular on the indigenous nationalities. The various Nepalese indigenous nationality groups have been raising their voices by identifying themselves as indigenous nationalities especially since the political change of 1990. One result of this has been the official recognition by the government itself. In this context, the Nepalese state has come to accept—even if implicitly—the multicultural reality of the Nepalese society. This has, one could argue, consequently struck at the monolithic nationalism created by the Nepalese state over the years.

If the early and mid-twentieth century had been the period of the metanarrative of nation building, development, etc., the time today is of "fragmentation," of the dissolution of old certainties. Groups like the indigenous nationalities have questioned the way the Nepalese state came to be made, pointing to their own exclusion and marginalisation. They have talked of federalism, autonomy and the division of the Nepalese state into "multi-nations." I have in this book attempted to look into the issues groups like the indigenous nationalities have raised, besides analysing their consequences for the future of the Nepalese state. Many of the issues the indigenous nationalities have raised in the Nepalese context have their resonance in a wider setting. Nepalese indigenous nationalities have also found their inspiration from the worldwide movement of indigenous peoples. The recent developments related to indigenous peoples in the international arena, such as the setting up of the United Nations Permanent Forum on Indigenous Issues and international instruments like the International Labour Organisation Convention No. 169 on Indigenous and Tribal Peoples and the United Nations Declaration on the Rights of Indigenous Peoples, have played their part in the issues being raised by Nepalese indigenous nationalities.

I attempt to look into the issues the indigenous nationalities have raised in the Nepalese context within a broader framework, as well as from a broader perspective. Although the issues have their own specificity, they are also part of the wider trends at the global level. I argue that the issues can be best understood in the context of a world in transition. A period of upheavals, an age of uncertainty can also be the time for the most feverish activity, even fecundity. Today, at a time of the decline of the West, a development trajectory begun a couple of centuries ago from a small corner of the world, namely the European continent is coming to an end. From a world that has been 'unipolar'—and I mean this not only in terms of political power but also with regard to intellectual and cultural influence—to a world whose contours are still being redrawn, these are times of transition, of flux.

This book is divided into eight chapters, including this introductory chapter. Chapter Two of the book focuses on the issue of what it means to be modern and the concept of modernity, while Chapter Three analyses the impact that modernity has had on the world, including in our own society. Chapter Four focuses on the current "revivalist" practices and the way non-Western peoples have begun to "talk back" to the West. Among these peoples are the Nepalese indigenous nationality groups. All this has struck at the metanarratives of modernity, such as progress and development, the nation-state, democracy, etc. Chapter Five of the book analyses the implications of the revivalist practices vis-à-vis the two grand narratives of democracy and nationalism. Chapter Six continues with the overall theme of Chapter Five, i.e. the malaise of modernity. Modernity's emphasis on human reason and its ambition to create a paradise on earth, in contradistinction to the heaven of ancient religions following death, have foundered against reality. The world today is multicultural, i.e. it is a world where the voices of diverse peoples and cultures can no longer be ignored and the West can no longer claim unopposed ascendancy amidst these varied ways of life. It is also a world that is interconnected or "globalised." The situation today brings forward challenges unlike those faced by human societies of the past, calling for solutions also unlike those of the past. Chapter Seven is an attempt to come forth with those solutions. Chapter Eight is the concluding section that ends this book.

2

Modernity and Its Contents

Referring to the present wave of globalisation, an observer has mentioned it as being the fourth wave of globalisation sweeping the world. The first wave of globalisation was the spread and universalisation of technology such as fire and of social institutions such as marriage, family, kinship and war. The second wave occurred with the spread of religions like Christianity, Hinduism, Buddhism and Islam. The third wave of globalisation was the universalisation of capital through colonialism and imperialism, while the most recent wave of globalisation is the universalisation of exploitation (Bhattachan 1996: 80-81).

The period around the beginning of the Christian era, what the philosopher Karl Jaspers has called the axial age and Samir Amin the tributary era, gave birth to the universalist concept of humanity. During the period stretching from the fifth century BC to the seventh century AD, the great religions of Zoroastrianism, Buddhism, Christianity and Islam were founded, and the great Confucian and Hellenistic philosophies were formulated. The common dimension and destiny of all human beings was thus affirmed, if only in the beyond. This declaration of an universalist vocation did not, of course, establish a real unification of humanity. The conditions of tributary society did not permit it, and humanity reformed itself into major tributary areas held together by their own particular universalist religion-philosophy (Christendom, Dar el Islam, the Hindu world, the Confucian world). In modern times, the bourgeois revolution initiated a second evolutionary wave that deepened and enriched the concept of universalism. The philosophy of the Enlightenment was the beginning of a movement that culminated in the French Revolution (Amin 1997: 80).

The present wave of globalisation nevertheless differs from the past in one important and fundamental respect. Although the propounders of religions like Buddhism and Christianity, as well as Islam, may well have aspired to a universal humanity, they remained constrained by the material conditions of life of their time. Today, with the almost incredible improvements in transportation and communication, the entire world has become interconnected in what is often referred to as the global village. Almost all parts of the world, including groups of peoples living in even the remotest corners of the globe, have come under the influence of what some would no doubt refer to as civilisation. This has led to the adoption by groups of peoples around the world of Western scientific innovations and technological knowhow, not to mention the aping of Western culture in the form of style, fashion and way of life.

The spread of Western influences has of course followed the ascendancy by the West itself. As the sun of the West rose in all its splendour, people around the world found it trendy being Western, being modern. And the capitalist production that accompanied the rise of the West meant that what were once regarded as luxuries within the reach of queens and emperors only, and not even within theirs occasionally, could now be accessible to a large mass of people. Capitalist mass production meant also production for the masses, and capitalism has made goods—the cheap cloth, the cheap cotton and rayon fabric, shoes, boots, motorcars and so on—accessible to the common men and women (Schumpeter 1954: 67). One consequence of this has been the increase in consumerism on an unprecedented scale—from the Rana rulers of the early twentieth century who had their private motorcar brought to the capital Kathmandu from the Nepal-India border carried on the shoulders of porters to the crass and unbridled consumerism of today.

Progress and Development

Nonetheless, if it was only consumerism that the West had given birth to, the history of the world might well have been different. The advances in science and technology in the West during the last couple of centuries, and the generation of knowledge accompanying these advances, have given rise to a particular way of looking at the world, namely the modern. And societies around the world, willy-nilly, have come under the impact of this modernity. This has happened with the availability of not only the "cheap" goods mentioned above, but also with the accessibility of medical services, modern educational facilities, electricity, transportation and communication services, one could add to this list considerably. There finds mention, in this context, of the Malla kings of the Nepal or Kathmandu Valley of the eighteenth century benefitting from the medical services provided by Western Capuchin missionaries. Today, of course, development has been elevated to a pedestal by itself, inspired by the modern idea of progress as something inevitable, even immanent in human nature. This ameliorative view of human society and human affairs, which is unique to modernity, continues to have a powerful impact on the discourse of our times.

Thus, leaders of developing, i.e. not yet fully "developed" countries like Nepal engage in periodic development planning, wax eloquent on development and, in general, go to great lengths to show to their people that they are wholeheartedly committed to development. Political leaders promise to 'do' development, to bring development or, in the words of the King-led Panchayat, to unleash the forces of development. Roads, schools, colleges and universities, hospitals, hydroelectric dams all become the symbols of this development, the new temples, so to say, of the gleamingly modern nation. (The seductiveness of development can be gauged from the fact that *bikas*, which is the Khas-Nepali word for development, has become particularly popular among Nepalese parents, who have named their sons as *Bikas*.)

The advance of modernisation and development has not been without its discontents, although it has been pretty relentless, as my use of the word willy-nilly above will also indicate. An indigenous nationality intellectual and activist has pointed to the "contradictory" nature of the impact of globalisation on Nepalese indigenous nationalities (Bhattachan

1996: 91). On the one hand, international human rights instruments, including those directly related to indigenous peoples, have provided the indigenous nationalities of Nepal the right to protect their societies and cultures. On the other, many elements of globalisation, along with the internal colonisation imposed by the dominant groups of the Nepalese society, have already destroyed these societies and cultures, some even to the point of extinction. In this context, the ambivalence towards the modern can also be seen from the comments of a well known Khas-Nepali literary figure. Writing around the middle of the twentieth century, the Khas-Nepali poet pointed to the "negative" consequences of the use of tables and chairs, in place of the traditional floor mat, as well as to the "harm" caused by clocks and watches. The poet, along with criticising the present, praised the past, nature, Hinduism, Sanskrit and the "ancient Aryan civilisation" (Devkota 1963/64: 24-25, 283-285).

This ambivalence or "anxiety" manifested itself among the Nepalese rulers as well. Although the Shah king Prithivi Narayan in the eighteenth century had evicted foreign merchants and banned the import of European goods, this was not followed by the rulers after him like the Ranas, forcing them instead to practice selective exclusion (Liechty 2008: 153). On the one hand, there were all the material comforts of a modern society like piped water, electric lighting, motor cars and communication services. From the import of British "broadcloth" for Nepalese military uniforms to the nobility's developing taste for foreign goods and styles, there was a significant increase in the consumption of European products in the nineteenth century. The Nepalese Prime Minister Bhimsen Thapa (1806-1837) was the first Nepalese leader to adopt a "purely western dress." By the 1830s, the whole of the Nepalese middle and upper classes were clad in foreign, i.e. British-made cottons and English cotton "chintzes" were much worn by the middle and lower classes. Only the "poor" still produced most of their own coarse cotton goods, though even among them English-made imitation South Asian textiles were making inroads. The Nepalese elites were not simply consuming foreign goods from sport rifles, glassware and crockery to mirrors, plate glass and lighting devices, but were also beginning to make significant concessions to foreign cultural practices. Bhimsen Thapa's "great glass palace" in Kathmandu was a combination of north Indian Mughal domes and minarets and European architectural styles. The increase in foreign goods and styles was tied to the flooding of Indian, and by extension Nepalese markets, with European goods following the end of the Napoleonic Wars. Following the establishment of the British Residency in 1816, the number of Indian merchants in Kathmandu dealing in European goods increased by a third, and local merchants estimated that between 1816 and 1831 trade volume tripled (Ibid.: 42-43).

Also, the rational ordering of time and space envisioned by modernity found among its starkest manifestations in the nation-state itself, with its concept of well-defined borders, territorial integrity and sovereignty, etc. And within these clearly demarcated boundaries rulers could effectively employ disciplinary and socialising technologies like army barracks, schools, colleges and educational institutions, hospitals and prisons with the aim of controlling, subverting and even exploiting their peoples. Thus, on the other hand, autocrats like the Rana rules were also anxious about maintaining control over all information about and representations of the outside world, prohibiting the movement of Nepalese or foreigners and tightly controlling books and newspapers (Ibid.: 153). The Ranas, therefore, went to great lengths to practice selective exclusion, or selective inclusion for that matter, vis-à-vis the modern.

The Modern Nation-State

The obsession with rational ordering of modernity led to the cold rationality of modern map making, to the modern maps which contrast with the tactile and sensual sense of medieval representation (Harvey 1989: 241-254). As capitalism with its emphasis on private property and private ownership became global, there was the need for delineating with detailed precision spatial boundaries. Maps served vital instrumental ends. After all, there were important natural resources to be tapped into and exploited, which could—and indeed did—lead to conflicts and even war. And, as these resources increasingly took on a "nationalist" form, there was the need for the precise demarcation of national boundaries.

The nation-state, like the idea of progress and development and bourgeois individualism, remains an uniquely modern phenomenon. An observer has pointed to the "frenzy of nations," the "frenzy of nationalism" that swept Europe in the nineteenth century.

> Before...most regions of the world were not yet consolidated into nations but were organized, rather, into a mishmash of tribes, clans, duchies, principalities, kingdoms, and other more or less local units. "Kings and princes"..."held power in bits and blobs." Borders were ill-defined, governmental rights fuzzy. The power of the state was not yet standardized. In one village...it amounted only to the right to collect tolls on a windmill, in another to tax the peasants, elsewhere to appoint an abbot. An individual with property in several different regions might owe allegiance to several lords. Even the greatest of emperors typically ruled over a patchwork of tiny locally-governed communities. Political power was not yet uniform. Voltaire summed it all up: In traveling across Europe, he complained, he had to change laws as frequently as horses....Yet without political integration, economic integration was impossible. Costly new...technologies could only be amortized if they produced goods for larger-than-local markets. But how could businessmen buy and sell over a large territory if, outside their own communities, they ran into a maze of different duties, taxes, labor regulations, and currencies? For the new technologies to pay off, local

> economics had to be consolidated into a single national economy. This meant a national division of labor and a national market for commodities and capital. All this, in turn, required national political consolidation as well (Toffler 1981: 80-81).

As societies began to build national economies, there was a fundamental shift in public consciousness. There was a gradual expansion in psychological horizons, as the number of people with a stake in the larger world beyond the local grew and multiplied. The new mass media increased the amount of information and imagery from beyond. Under the impact of these changes, national consciousness stirred and localism faded (Ibid.).*

---

* As Alvin Toffler says: "The small-scale local production…had bred a race of highly provincial people—most of whom concerned themselves exclusively with their own neighborhoods or villages. Only a tiny handful—few nobles and churchmen, a scattering of merchants, and a social fringe of artists, scholars, and mercenaries—had interests beyond the village….With steam- and coal-based technologies, and later with the advent of electricity, it became possible for a manufacturer of clothing in Frankfurt, watches in Geneva, or textiles in Manchester to produce far more units than the local market could absorb. He also needed raw materials from afar. The factory worker, too, was affected by financial events occurring thousands of miles away: jobs depended on distant markets….Starting with the American and French revolutions and continuing through the nineteenth century, a frenzy of nationalism swept across the industrializing part of the world. Germany's three hundred and fifty petty diverse quarrelling mini-states needed to be combined into a single national market—das Vaterland. Italy—broken into pieces and ruled variously by the House of Savoy, the Vatican, the Austrian Hapsburgs, and the Spanish Bourbons—had to be united. Hungarians, Serbs, Croats, Frenchmen, and others all suddenly developed mystical affinities for their fellows. Poets exalted the national spirit. Historians discovered long-lost heroes, literature, and folklore. Composers wrote hymn to nationhood. All at precisely the moment when industrialization made it necessary" (Toffler 1981: 80-81).

The process of integrating far flung areas into a national whole accompanied the improvements in transportation and communication. The industrialising countries of Europe and North America were helped in this by one of the technological advances of the nineteenth century, the transportation miracle of the time, namely the railway. Railway lines were laid joining different parts of a country, including in the United States where the railway in the nineteenth century joined the Atlantic with the Pacific. A country the size of a continent like the United States could be welded into a nation through the railway, and the government could quickly mobilise its army all over the country to assert its "national" authority. We can compare the situation in Europe and the United States with our own, albeit the century in our case is the twentieth and not the nineteenth and the means of transport is the road and not the railway.

As national "frenzy" reached non-Western countries like Nepal in the twentieth century, poets and writers, not to mention politicians, of those countries strove to imagine "a new community." Thus, with this aim in mind, King Mahendra in the early 1960s at the beginning of the Panchayat inaugurated the construction of the East-West highway. The highway joining the eastern part of Nepal with the western along the tarai or the plains in the south was to perform the urgent and important task of national integration. It would forge a common national identity by bringing together the people of the different parts of the country. Road building continues to remain an important development activity even today, as the Nepalese state attempts to extend its reach to the farthest corners of the country.

Uniformity and Standardisation

The industrialisation of the economy along with the improvements in transportation and communication joined the far lying areas and hinterlands to the centre, along with the people living therein. This brought uniformity in behaviour, creating a common set of standards for the majority of the population. Industrialisation gave birth to the massified society, where a large number of people followed the same pattern in their daily lives. This was dictated by the need to maintain and follow a strict timetable at the workplace. The "office time" of the workplace imposed its own routine also at the home, where eating, sleeping and other daily activities had to be carefully synchronised with the time that had to be spent at the workplace. As the rhythm of machines established a working day measured in hours and paid by hours worked, time became money. It differed from the rhythm imposed by the farmer's seasons, the sun, the weather and the needs of the farm's animals. It differed also from the working rhythm of the home weavers, to whom not time but their finished output was money (Rosenberg and Birdzell, Jr. 1987: 149). Unlike traditional agricultural societies where punctuality and being on time is not terribly important, primarily because agricultural work is not highly interdependent, there is enormous cultural pressure to assure punctuality in modern ones. In modern societies, one worker's lateness can immediately and dramatically disrupt the work of many others in the factory or the office (Toffler 1981: 253).

The mass society with the frequent interaction of a large number of people led to the imposition of uniformity with regard to the acceptable behaviour in the society. The masses of people were required to conform to an entire set of behavioural rules. There were, along with the strict timetable and the norms of punctuality to be adhered to at the workplace, a whole range of activities like dress codes to be followed, table manners to be maintained, traffic rules to be given regard to, etc. Even such apparently inconsequential physical activities like the disposing of saliva, coughing and sneezing came to be strictly regulated by the larger society. The industrialised mass society's strict imposition of behavioural codes of conduct has, of course, led to the allegation that it creates faceless and nameless citizenry chained to the drab monotony of life.

As regards the Nepalese context, although industrialisation in the country even at the turn of the twenty-first century remains more of a slogan than a reality, another kind of uniformity, standardisation or homogenisation has been at work. This is the one imposed by the Nepalese state in its attempts to build a 'nation' out of what is an incredibly diverse society. This attempt reached its apogee in the 'Panchayati nationalism' or the 'Mahendra nationalism,' called so after King Mahendra who ended multiparty democracy in the country and imposed the partyless Panchayat system in 1960. The Panchayat constructed a nationalism based on ethnicity, even 'race,' around a so-called *Nepali jati*, i.e. a single and uniform and homogenous Nepalese people, Nepalese nation or even Nepalese 'race,' speaking the same language (Khas-Nepali), and sharing the same religion (Hindu) and same culture (Hindu).

Nepal, like so many other non-Western and non-industrialised societies around the world in the twentieth century, entered its "nationalist" phase without the rapid industrialisation and the consequent mass societies seen in the West. Nepalese communists tend to see Nepal as a semi-feudal, as well as a semi-colonial, country. This despite the fact that Nepal's political economy has changed dramatically during the course of the last half century. Nepal at the end of the Rana family rule in 1951 had a state structure that was feudal, with the government's primary revenue coming from land taxation. Today, land revenues amount to less than one percent of the state's income, the bulk of which comes from import duties. Thus, the Nepalese state is no longer ruled by feudals. It has passed, especially since the 1980s, into the hands of the trading class comprador bourgeoisie (Gyawali 2003: 230). Nevertheless, Nepalese communists, like the other political forces of the country, have been able to successfully mobilise the Nepalese people by raising nationalist slogans and whipping up nationalist sentiments for around the last fifty years.

The National Project

The nation building project in non-Western developing countries has closely followed the path of the West. The intellectuals and political leaders of developing countries may well have fought their liberation struggles against the West and railed against what they perceived as Western colonialism and imperialism, but these intellectuals and political leaders when they became free from the shackles of Western rule have aspired to the very nationalist model propounded by the West. Nationalism, national right to self-determination, national self-government, national sovereignty and territorial integrity and their inviolability, all key concepts associated with the modern nation-state, have been crucial to the discourse of the intellectuals and political leaders of developing countries. And, as their Western counterparts, the "nation builders" of developing countries have also superimposed upon what have traditionally been diverse societies a monolithic nationalism centred around one culture, one language, one dress, etc.

In Nepal, the nationalist model, and the accompanying imposition of uniformity and the negating of differences, has taken on a distinctly Hindu form. This has happened with the attempts by the Nepalese ruling Hindu "high" caste groups to make Nepal an *asali Hindustan*, i.e. the true and pure land of the Hindus. The constitutional status of Nepal as a 'Hindu state' ended only recently with the declaration by the House of Representatives of May 18, 2006 of Nepal as a secular state, something that has been given continuity in the Interim Constitution of Nepal 2007. With Hinduism traditionally accorded the status of a 'national religion,' the laws of the state have been based on Hindu religious and cultural practices. This has led to the propagation and the spread of Hindu norms and values throughout the Nepalese society.

Among the most important, as well as one of the most insidious, impact of Hinduism in the Nepalese society has been the caste system. The Nepalese state attempted to impose a "national caste system" all over Nepal with the National Legal Code (*Muluki Ain*) of 1854. The Code ascribed to the different groups in the Nepalese society, including various indigenous nationality groups, their specific roles in the Hindu caste hierarchy. In this hierarchy the ruling Hindu caste groups of Bahun, Thakuri and Chhetri were accorded the highest status as *tagadhari* or the wearers of the holy cord. Below them were the ruled of the Nepalese society, the various indigenous nationality groups, called by the Code as *matawali* or alcohol drinkers, some of whom could even be enslaved as punishment, as well as the "impure" and "untouchable" castes, i.e. the *dalit* (Serchan 2007: 14-15). The National Legal Code of 1854 provided for legislation on commensality and physical contact, with ritually prescribed codes of behaviour for and between the different groups. The insidious impact of the Code upon the society can be seen from the fact that caste-based discrimination and untouchability persist in the Nepalese society to this day even in the twenty-first century.

Along with the Hindu norms and values pervading the Nepalese state, the language of the rulers—Khas-Nepali—became another medium for imposing uniformity throughout the society. The language historically known as *Khaskura, Parbate, Gorkha,* etc. was rechristened by the Nepalese state as 'Nepali,' that is as the national language of all Nepal and all Nepalese peoples. In this regard, one can see two kinds of uniformity and standardisation at work. One is the imposition of uniformity within the language in attempts to create a 'standard' Khas-Nepali language. This led to the acceptance of one particular variant of the language, along with its propagation throughout the society, while at the same time marginalising all the other variants as "dialects," i.e. not a full-fledged language proper. The other is the imposition of uniformity without, as Khas-Nepali as the language of all the groups of peoples in the Nepalese society. This led to the "banishing" and the marginalisation by the Nepalese state of the around one hundred other languages of the country, languages belonging to not only the Tibeto-Burman, Dravidian and Munda families but also the Indo-European, of which the Khas-Nepali language is a branch.

The Nepalese state in the process of creating a modern nation-state attempted to construct several "national" symbols. These symbols, given their very national character, were supposed to represent all the diverse groups of the Nepalese society. They were, in fact, representative of the ruling groups in the Nepalese society. Some of them were associated with the Hindu king, in a Hindu state, such as the crown, sceptre, royal crest and the royal standard. Others were associated with an aspiring modern Nepalese nation-state, such as the triangular national flag based on the Hindu religion, the national coat-of-arms, national animal (the sacred animal of the Hindus the cow), national bird (pheasant), national flower (rhododendron), national colour (red colour, *simrik*), national festivals (the Hindu festivals of *Dashain, Tihar*, etc.) and the state-sanctioned national holidays associated with these festivals, and the national dress (*daura suruwal* for men and *sari* for women). Some of these national symbols like the cow, rhododendron, pheasant and red colour have found continuation in the Interim Constitution of Nepal 2007. In this context, the cow even today continues to remain sacrosanct, and the harsh laws related to the killing and eating of cows, i.e. twelve years in jail remain in effect even after the declaration of the Nepalese state as secular.

As the Nepalese state extended its bureaucracy and bureaucratic structures all over the country, the remote and outlying regions of the country also increasingly came under its influence. The Nepalese state constructed temples for Hindu gods and goddesses in offices, hospitals and in schools, colleges and university established around the country. The particular culture and way of life of the dominant ruling groups of the Nepalese society came to be 'universalised,' and set forth as the standard as the national culture and way of life. This homogenising nationalism led to the destruction of differences and to the imposition of uniformity throughout the society. The dress codes, the food habits of the ruling groups, such as the consumption of the meat of the castrated male goat (*khasi*), in contrast to buffalo meat, pork or beef, came to be seen as the standard. The eating of rice—or "rice culture"—came to permeate the entire society, even the remote hills and the mountains where crops like millet, maize and buckwheat have traditionally been the staple diet and rice remains a scarcity, a luxury. The way the Nepalese state came to impose itself upon the society can be seen from the comments with regard to "Belaspur," a small town and district headquarter of the country.

> The rhythm of daily life in Belaspur Bazaar is to a very large degree determined by the district administration. Men employed in its offices must complete a whole round of activities—bathing, breakfasting, visiting, even cultivating—before leaving for work. Shopkeepers adjust their opening hours to those of the administration, for many of their regular customers are government servants who make their small but regular purchases of cigarettes, betel nut, etc. on the way to their offices. At the end of the working day, the main street of the town, quiet save for a handful of visitors or shoppers during office hours (10 am-4 or 5 pm, depending on the season), fills with civil servants....On Saturdays, when government offices are shut, most shops close down as well, and a stillness settles on the town; it appears deserted....But setting a tempo is not the only way in which the district administration imposes itself upon the town. For one thing it is and has been for many years a major influence on the occupational and general economic position of those who live in the bazaar (Caplan 1975: 29).

Being Modern in Modernity

Before ending this chapter, it might be well to recapitulate the views and arguments presented so far. Thus, we find that with the ascendancy of the West and with the improvements in transportation and communication modernity, i.e. the modern way of looking at things has become truly global. Even the remote regions of the world, the most outlying areas of the planet have come under the impact of the modern.

The roots of modernity, in the way we use the term today, can be traced to the eighteenth century European Enlightenment. The *philosophes* of the Age of Enlightenment declared that the modern, post-medieval civilisation, based supremely on Reason with a capital R, was superior to the ancient and the ancient world. In this context, modernity refers to the social order that emerged following the Enlightenment. The modern world is marked by its unprecedented dynamism, its dismissing or marginalising of tradition and by its global consequences. In the modern world time seemed to speed up and space to open up. Modernity's forward-looking thrust relates strongly to the belief in progress and the power of human reason to produce freedom (Lyon 2002: 25).

What are the characteristics of this modernity, of this particular way of perceiving things, of looking at the world that had its roots in a particular place and time but which today has become global? Along with its belief in reason to solve all problems, there are some characteristics that can be regarded as uniquely modern. Paraphrasing John Gray, we can point to three major characteristics of modernity. It is *individualist*, in that it asserts the moral primacy of the person or the individual against the claims of any social collectivity, any group. It is *universalist*, in as much as it affirms the moral unity of the human species and accords a secondary importance to specific historic associations and cultural forms. And it is *meliorist*, in that it affirms the corrigibility and improvability of all social institutions and political arrangements (Gray 1998: xii). The "project" of modernity amounts to an extraordinary intellectual effort on the part of Enlightenment thinkers to develop objective science, universal morality and law and autonomous art according to their inner logic (Harvey 1989: 13). The aim was to use the accumulation of knowledge generated by many individuals working freely and creatively for the pursuit of human emancipation and the enrichment of daily life. The scientific domination of nature promised freedom from scarcity, want and arbitrariness of natural calamity. The development of rational forms of social organisation and rational modes of thought promised liberation from the irrationalities of myth, religion, superstition and release from the arbitrary use of power as well as the dark side of our human natures. Enlightenment thought embraced the idea of progress and actively sought that break with history and tradition which modernity espouses. It was above all a secular movement that sought the demystification and desacralisation of knowledge and social organisation in order to liberate human beings from their chains. In this context, doctrines of equality, liberty, faith in human intelligence (once allowed the benefits of education) and universal reason abounded. There was the optimism that the arts and sciences would promote not only the control of natural forces but also the understanding of the world and of the self, moral progress, the justice of institutions and even the happiness of human being (Ibid.).

Modernity's emphasis on human reason, its belief in the idea of progress, its individualist creed and its universalist pretensions are coming under increasing attack today. A number of these attacks stem from the inconsistencies and contradictions inherent in modernity itself. Thus, modernity has been referred to as "that enticingly packaged if internally inconsistent combination of instrumental rationality, utilitarianism and respect for individual autonomy and choice" (Khilnani 1994: 190). Modernity, despite its claims to universality, also gave rise to the strident particularism of the nation-state. Nevertheless, despite its inconsistencies internally, modernity was—and still remains, admittedly—an "enticing package" for numerous groups and millions of peoples around the world. Has this enticement been purely due to the fact that the West, i.e. the cradle of modernity has been ascendant for the last couple of centuries? It is after all human nature to aspire for, even ape, the dominant culture of the time. And with the inevitable decline and even demise of the West, will modernity itself, with not only its contradictions and inconsistencies but also its achievements, also fade from human consciousness and memory? In the chapters that follow I attempt to delve into these issues. I look into the inconsistencies and contradictions associated with modernity, as well as the impact they are having vis-à-vis modernity's long term prospects. While doing so, I focus in particular on the Nepalese context, and especially on the Nepalese indigenous nationalities, although the conclusions I arrive at can be applicable to a larger context.

3

The Modern Experience: Impact and Consequences

The *philosophes* of the Age of Enlightenment harboured extraordinary and extravagant hopes of human reason. The seventeenth century mathematician and philosopher Gottfried Leibniz had dreamed of a system of logic so compelling that it would resolve not only all mathematical questions but also philosophical, moral and political ones. Leibniz had believed in an "irrefutable calculus" that would solve all problems even theological ones (Horgan 1997: 207, 304).

The rational optimism in human perfectibility, in the power of reason to come forth with solutions to all problems, in control and dominion over nature, in linear progress and in the future that would not resemble the present but would be, in fact, a fundamental break with, as well as an improvement upon, the present as well as the past characterise Enlightenment thinking. Not only was the march of progress relentless, with the human condition only getting better and better with every passing day, but such progress would be universal, ultimately encompassing the entire world, unifying it one single whole. Thus, it was in this spirit that the nineteenth century French poet and novelist Victor Hugo predicted an "extraordinary nation" of the future that would have as its capital Paris but would no longer be called France. It would be called Europe, and in the centuries that followed, still further transformed, it would be called "Humanity," thus encompassing the entire world and all its peoples.

Universalism's Paradox

Poets, writers, thinkers and philosophers, as well as the propounders of various religious faiths, have in the past conceived of a liberating vision for all of humanity that would encompass the entire world. The vision is liberating given that, in principle, it recognises the equal moral worth of all human beings and advocates that the benefits accruing to one be within the reach of all. In a world divided along various lines, and where these divisions have been the basis for discrimination and exploitation, if not much worse, to conceive of equality without any exceptions has to be considered progressive. These egalitarian ideals can have particular resonance for the traditionally oppressed groups of the Nepalese society like the indigenous nationalities and of course the *dalit*. For the *dalit* not only in Nepal but also in the larger South Asian context, the emphasis on their common humanity with others remains among the major pillars of their struggles.

In a society like Nepal where hierarchical divisions based on the Hindu religion, as well as the inhuman practices associated with them like untouchability, have been sanctioned and propagated through laws like the National Legal Code of 1854, egalitarian principles applicable to all universally will have their appeal. Thus, modern Nepalese constitutions have enshrined under fundamental rights the right to equality, stating that all citizens shall be equal before the law and that no person shall be denied the equal protection of the laws. The State shall not discriminate among its citizens on the basis of religion, race, caste, ethnicity or ideological conviction, and no discrimination shall be carried out against any citizen in the application of general laws on the basis of the same. Also, while referring to the nation, Nepalese constitutions like the Constitution of the Kingdom of Nepal 1990 have mentioned that all the Nepalese people, irrespective of their religion, race, caste or ethnicity, collectively constitute the nation.

The emphasis on individual equality and the eradication and elimination of differences arising from ethnicity, caste, colour, race, religion, language, sex, birth, origin, etc. have been seen, not unjustifiably, as an emancipatory project, given the fact that discrimination, deprivation and exploitation based on the same have been a permanent feature during the course of human history. The emphasis on a common and universal humanity and equal moral worth of all has been a liberating ideal through history. But it has to be remembered here that there are two kinds of differences: those that are sources of inequality in society and those that protect and nourish creativity. By emphasising on a universal human individuality and by ignoring cultural differences, the idea of formal equality treats unequals equally (Mahajan 1998: 1, 7).

Of course, the claims to universality, by suppressing all kinds of differences, by themselves lead to the imposition of homogeneity and the stamping out of diversity. Thus, when "world religions" like Buddhism, Christianity and Islam aspire to universality, it is an universality based on homogeneity. In other words, these respective faiths want the rest of the world to convert and resemble them, hence leading to assimilation and homogenisation. Liberal modernity, based on the "fiction of abstract individuality," emphasises on a particular way of life and claims it as universal. The liberal individual, divested of all historical and cultural contexts, exists unmediated between himself or herself and the universe. Any mediation would only confirm the fiction of liberal universality. Instead of being universal, however, the emphasis on individuality has its roots in a particular time and place, namely England of the seventeenth century where the language and theory of the protection of human rights developed. The issue at the time was seen as one of deprivation because of conscience, because of individual decision and action, rather than one of deprivation due to race, colour or national origin. England was relatively homogenous, except for religion and political attitudes which largely flowed from religious conviction. These were seen as individual decisions, and protecting diversity was seen as an issue of protecting the diversity that flowed from individual decisions (Glazer 1998: 419).

Modernity's claims to universality presuppose assimilation and the obliterating of differences. To be universal, therefore, is to be one. Although Enlightenment theorists in England and France noted the existence of plural cultures and civilisations around the world, in keeping with their understanding of plurality, they arranged these cultures hierarchically (Mahajan 1999). Natural Eurocentric bias led to the grading of western culture as superior to the rest. All this would lead to the "white man's burden," to theories of racism, colonialism and Social Darwinism justifying the exploitation and the plunder and pillage of the rest of the world. Westerners might well have seen non-Western societies existing in a Hobbesian state of nature "solitary, poor, nasty, brutish and short" that had to be brought under the civilising influence of the West. It is not surprising in this context that much of Western thinking has been assimilationistic. This includes nineteenth century thinking, among which comprise such supposedly liberal and progressive thinkers from John Stuart Mill to Karl Marx. Marx eulogised about the historic, positive, progressive and civilising role played by capital, welcoming the American victory over Mexico in the war of 1846-48 and supporting the British "mission," i.e. colonial rule in India. Marx saw the British "mission" in India as a double mission: "the annihilation of the old Asiatic society and the laying of the material foundations of Western society in India" (Hobsbawm 1992: 161.). Marx, along with Mill and other thinkers of the time, had disregard, even contempt, for the "small peoples" and minority cultures around the world.

As a product of his time, Marx saw humanity and the human society progressing in stages, epochs or eras. Unlike some of the other bourgeois thinkers of his time, however, Marx conceived of the ultimate stage of humanity as a state-less and property-less communist utopia, where humans would live finally escaping from the world of necessity to the world of freedom. The belief in progress leads, of course, to the inevitable hierarchical grading of peoples, cultures and civilisations, not only through time but also across space. Societies other than one's own can come to be judged and even stereotyped as un-progressive, undeveloped and uncivilised. In this context, modernity's future-oriented emphasis on progress and its "obsessional enmity" to the past, to tradition and convention have meant that words like ancient, old, traditional have by themselves come to bear a negative connotation in our times.

Nepalese Modernity and Development

Today, of course, the concepts of progress and development have by themselves become universal. Countries around the world like Nepal, if they are not developed, are said to be developing, that is on the path to being fully developed. The trajectory of development to be followed by these supposedly developing countries is the one retroactively applied to the already "developed" countries of the West. Thus, the aim is to create numerous "Wests" around the world modelled on "the West." The indicators used to measure development are modern ones, viz. literacy, education, concrete housing, urbanisation, access to services as roads and transportation and communication services, electricity, piped water, modern health facilities, etc. And, of course, with the ascribing to a particular way of life as the standard and claiming it as universal, comes the inevitable negating, marginalisation, exclusion and the stereotyping of all other ways of life. At present, although the development discourse may be more nuanced than in the past, for instance instead of primitive the word pre-literate may be used. Nevertheless, these so-called pre-literate peoples are still expected to acquire the modern amenities and undergo the technological advances the West has gone through in the last couple of centuries.

Modernity privileges the town over the village, the urban over the rural, the "written" over the "oral" and the industrialised over the agrarian as developed and progressive. Marx himself (along with Freidrich Engles) in the *Communist Manifesto* had written about the "idiocy" of rural life. Later, V.I. Lenin declared that the country, i.e. the rural areas cannot be equal to the town. Under the historical conditions of the epoch, the town inevitably leads the rural areas, and the rural areas inevitably follow the town (Lenin 1965: 257). Both Marx and Lenin, as well as other communists, have seen the urban industrialised working class as a revolutionary, i.e. progressive force, while at the same time labelling the rural agricultural workers as reactionary. Given modernity's emphasis on the urban, it is not surprising that Nepalese desperate to be modern are eager to convert their villages into "towns" and "municipalities" and earn recognition from the government as such. When such recognition has not been forthcoming, they often make do by declaring their villages as "town-oriented" villages. This despite the fact that in many of these "town-oriented" villages and even the towns and municipalities the issue is not of vehicular parking but of controlling stray cattle, or of farmers drying their grains on roads that can lead to traffic accidents.

The denigrating of the rural way of life becomes evident from the use of the Khas-Nepali word *Pakhe*. The word which derives from the Khas-Nepali word *Pakha* meaning the side of a hill has come to acquire a pejorative connotation in the Nepalese society. It refers to the villager, the "country bumpkin" unaccustomed to the urban way of life. Thus, the word *Pakhe* means not modern, not urban, un-cool and even uncivilised and uncouth. Many jokes abound in the Nepalese society of the village bumpkin unaccustomed to the town, the city and the urban way of life.

In this context, the contrast between the urban and the rural can manifest itself even in the choice of sports. For instance, while volleyball has traditionally been popular among rural youths, the preferred sport among the "hip" urban youths is basketball. The privileging of the urban over the rural means that it is not only the games you play, or what you wear and how you speak that determine your life chances, but the skills that you acquire can also advance or retard your chances in life. And as globalisation continues to encroach further and further into the rural hinterlands, the rural way of life and the skills—technical as well as otherwise—associated with the way of life, are made redundant by the new forces of the market. The locals are also caught up in globalisation's paradox, as they attempt to globalise they are beaten by the globalists.

A historian has pointed to the Anglo-Nepal treaty of 1923 that led to the flooding of the local market with foreign goods destroying the rural cottage industries of the country. The treaty, which formally recognised Nepal's independence, extended to the Nepalese government the right to import through India any weapons and ammunition needed for the well being of Nepal. Also, trade goods imported by Nepalese merchants from third countries would pay customs duty in Kolkota. If the consignment was shipped to Nepal without breaking bulk and arrived in Kathmandu with the customs seals intact, the duty paid was to be refunded. This last facility delighted the Nepalese merchants, but proved a mixed blessing to the people. A rash of Japanese products flooded the Kathmandu market, overflowed into the hills and the tarai and threatened to seep across the border into India. Many Nepalese veterans from World War I had cash, which they spent freely to celebrate their safe return, happy in being able to buy modern goods for their families. Nepal's thriving cottage industries were killed. The money the veterans had brought back to the villages, which might have financed a boom in the rural economy, was dissipated (Stiller 1989: 113).

As the forces of globalisation have continued their encroachment apace, they have proven the death knell of the local. Local cottage industries like the weaving of home-made cotton as well as woollen clothes have been displaced by imported clothing, locally made pots, pans and other utensils have been superseded by plastic and steel goods from outside and local technologies used for the grinding of grains, pressing of oil like watermill, etc. have been overtaken by modern diesel-powered mills. Even a typically local "artistic" item—the example given is of a particular type of jug (*karuwa*) produced in Palpa district of the western hills—is displaced, as outside industries produce the same item of the same quality on a mass scale, with which the local industries simply cannot compete (Blaikie et al. 1980: 189).

The prevailing worldview or the dominant discourse privileges a particular way of life—the stable and sedentary vis-à-vis the mobile and nomadic, the modern vis-à-vis the pastoralist, etc.—over others. It denigrates other ways of life and systematically undermines and destroys other knowledge systems in order to achieve and maintain its hegemony. Groups like the indigenous nationalities and their way of life are regarded as unsustainable and not viable, and stereotyped and discriminated against by this prevailing worldview.

> Many African indigenous groups face discrimination and negative stereotyping, depicting them as underdeveloped and uncivilised. The dominant development paradigms..., focusing on agricultural development and "modern" sectors, contribute to fostering such prejudice and lack of readiness to consider other forms of production and land use positively. Recent research has shown that the modes of production of pastoralists and hunter-gatherers and their unique adaptations to the natural surroundings offer sustainability and long-term success in desert, savannah, forest, wetland and mountainous areas. These people are often contributing substantially to the national economy as well. All this is often ignored and not even known or realised by national authorities (Jensen 2003: 4).

The theory of the "tragedy of the commons" is just one aspect of how pastoralism is viewed in the dominant discourse. The dominant discourse, being a Western discourse, has nothing to say on pastoral development or accumulation based on pastoral livestock production. It is simply not in the "holy books." The dominant discourse and the "holy books" from Adam Smith to numerous other economists simply do not recognise it. However, pastoral accumulation is not only a possibility but can even be more feasible and contribute more to the national economy than other traditional economies (Tegegn 2003: 35). Thus, the challenge before us is

> to develop appropriate models of development through which hunter-gatherer communities can enjoy equal opportunities in health care, education, employment, land and justice without loss of culture and identity. Unfortunately, the dominant

> models of development are essentially assimilationist, for example requiring mobile communities to sedentarise so that they can obtain identity cards, send their children to school, live in modern housing and so on. Forest peoples' organisations urgently need information about alternative development models, including for example, ambulant education using curricula which teach children about important aspects of their culture and livelihoods; modernisation of traditional skills such as hunting, gathering, use of herbal remedies; and appropriate land tenure systems combining land security with scope for practicing traditional livelihoods (Jackson 2003: 12).

The prevailing modern worldview has difficulty accepting alternative perspectives regarding property, land and other resources. It has difficulty reconciling with the indigenous and tribal concept of land as territory and not property. Thus, disregarding the concept of land prevailing among indigenous peoples, it can declare indigenous lands as *terra nullius*, i.e. lands belonging to no one and confiscate them. The nineteenth century French writer Alexis de Tocqueville wrote that the Native Americans, i.e. the indigenous peoples of North America occupied but did not posses the land, given that it is by agriculture that man wins the soil. In this context, one wonders what Tocqueville would say today about the contemporary capitalist form that is now nomadic in finance, trade, management, communication and travel and has left agriculture in the Tocquevillian sense far behind (Connolly 2000: 188). Another nineteenth century intellectual, the "liberal" John Stuart Mill, stated that nothing but foreign force would induce a tribe of Native Americans to submit to the restraints of a regular and civilised government. Liberal modernity, given that the boundaries of liberal individuality, rights and justice are set in advance by its parameters of the liberal nation, has difficulty negotiating new forms of property, freedom and rights involving patterns of land use and ownership at odds with the image of the nation which it begins. This connection between the liberal nation and the shape of the individuality not only encourages liberal thinkers to misread the past violences upon which construction of a nation is based, but it also sets the stage for later struggles within liberalism itself over the limits to diversity in the liberal state (Ibid.).

As regards the Nepalese context, a particular type of land system mentioned of the indigenous nationalities of the country is the *kipat*. The *kipat*, a communal land system, was found among various indigenous nationality groups of the country (see Serchan 2001: 67-68). According to the system, which regulated the relationship of the indigenous nationality group to the environment, land was distributed according to need, and if a family had more land than it needed, the land was allocated to others in need. Also, the prevailing indigenous nationality organisation controlled fodder and fuel-collecting rights, and imposed rules allocating certain amount of land for grazing so that over-grazing would not result (Poffenberger 1980: 51-52). The *kipat* system came to an end with the arrival of the Bahun, Chhetri and Thakuri with a different cultural background and perspective towards the land and the environment, and who preferred such statutory land tenure systems as the *Birta* land grant system. The Nepalese government dominated by these hill Hindu "high" caste groups oversaw the transformation of the communally-owned *kipat* lands into government-administered *raikar* lands, with the *kipat* system coming to an end with the Land Reform Act of 1964.

Although it may not be obviously apparent to the modern "blinkered" by its notions of development and its ethnocentric biases, alternative ways of life can be good and beneficial and advantageous in their own ways. An anthropologist points to how the hunting and gathering period of human existence provided the best fed and the healthiest humans in the history of our species (Fisher 1987: 38). And unlike what some might think, the level of violence within and between hunting and gathering cultures appears generally to have been quite low, and there were no specialised warriors in those cultures. With the appearance of armed soldiery, the situation became different. Most agrarian states were based in a very direct way upon military power. Yet in such states the monopoly of control of the means of violence on the part of the ruling authorities was always far from complete. Such states were never internally pacified by the standards of today's modern nation-states, with the latter's control of the means of violence, surveillance, etc. (Giddens 1990).

Nepal's own hunter-gatherers the indigenous nationality group Raute numbering in the hundreds, too, have had to suffer from stigmatisation from being perceived as "backward." The Raute's nomadic lifestyle in the forests, their appearance and their cultural habits, including the fact that they hunt and eat monkeys, can be fodder for exotica, if not outright stereotyping. The pressure borne on the Raute to conform to the so-called mainstream, in this context, can be overwhelming, with scant consideration given to the Raute's own views on the matter. The semi-autonomous government body of the National Foundation for Development of Indigenous Nationalities, a body which is headed by an indigenous nationality intellectual/activist appointed by the government, not only brought some Rautes, along with some other individuals belonging to various indigenous nationality groups, to the capital Kathmandu but also took them on a tour around the country. Some indigenous nationality activists under the aegis of the Foundation even went to the traditional area of the Raute, the mid-western hills, to provide "assistance" to them. These enthusiasts when the Raute, in an indication perhaps of the sign of the times, refused to take anything in kind instead preferring payment in money, had to provide their "assistance" in cash.

The dominant "mainstream" discourse can regard the way of life of groups like the indigenous nationalities as deviant, as essentially lacking or being inadequate in something. Hence, for this dominant discourse not only the Raute but also indigenous nationality groups like the Chepang living in caves and not in modern housing are evidences of this "lack" or "inadequacy." The dominant discourse considers the way of life of indigenous nationalities as inferior. It fails to appreciate the traditional egalitarian beliefs and value systems of indigenous peoples as well as the indigenous notion of community, justice and the regulated use of one's surrounding natural resources. This assertion of superiority leads to the marginalisation and ultimately the destruction of alternative ways of life. The evolvement of political hegemony in countries like Nepal means that the way of life and systems such as that of indigenous nationality groups based on balanced reciprocity are likely to be increasingly undermined by the growth of accumulative strategies of economic practice, many of which are promoted as "development" (Holmberg 1996: 76). An economy of the market based on the profit motive gives rise to norms and values often contrary to those of groups like the indigenous nationalities.

The anthropologist Christoph von Furer-Haimendorf, for instance, has pointed to the impact the growth of tourism and the accompanying money economy has had on the indigenous nationality group the Sherpa. As the Sherpa travelled beyond their traditional homelands and as the old values of a society virtually free of competition and rivalry no longer fit an economic system that encourages individuals to consider the acquisition of money as their first priority, this has transformed the Sherpa. Even the practice of visiting one another by going to each other's house has been impacted among the Sherpa with their strong sense of community as well as hospitality. As the houses may be occupied by paying foreign tourists, the Sherpa have become less inclined to visit each other for a chat and a drink. The increased emphasis on money has also brought about a change in the way the Sherpa have traditionally viewed wealth. In the past, wealth was not desired for its own sake but as a means for providing adequate food and clothing for the household, with sufficient surplus to entertain guests as often and lavishly as possible. It was also valued because it enabled a person to dispense charity and give donations to religions institutions, thereby acquiring merit (Furer-Haimendorf 1984: 69, 112).

As *Homo sapiens* are seen primarily as *Homo economicus*, things in life can come to be regarded in purely monetary terms or, as an anthropologist puts it, as an accountant's balance sheet (Caplan 2000: 209). An indigenous nationality displaced from his or her traditional lands due to "development" activities like the construction of hydroelectric dams, roads, etc. can therefore be easily "compensated" in cash. This is despite the fact that the indigenous nationality individual may have lived on the land for centuries, if not millennia, and working the land may be the only form of employment he or she knows. (There is also the fact that indigenous peoples not only have material but also spiritual relationships with their ancestral lands.) Uprooted from the only environment he or she knows, the indigenous nationality is thrust helpless amidst the forces of the market. He or she is expected overnight to learn the ways of the market and adjust himself or herself accordingly, even in a sustainable way. Instead, the indigenous nationality individual concerned may spend the money received in compensation in activities like the consumption of alcohol, leading ultimately to pauperisation.

The Market and Globalisation

Market globalisation would obviously want all groups and peoples all over the world to conform to its strictures, thus integrating the entire world in one unified whole. The proponents of this globalisation expect all peoples to behave with what they regard as economic rationality. For these proponents the earth is flat, and people all over the world irrespective of their culture, language, ethnicity and region have equal access to the benefits of the market and globalisation. Groups like the indigenous nationalities are, therefore, expected to shed their "irrationality" and follow the rules of the market and globalisation. They are even expected to take up the 'Protestant ethic,' and its "emphasis on thrift, unremitting toil and the deferral of gratification," traits by which the West is said to have channelled enormous energies into the tasks of economic development during the last couple of centuries. Thus, globalisation entails homogenisation and, ultimately for the vast majority of peoples unable to swim in its tide, sinking in marginalisation.

The uneven nature of globalisation can be seen from Nepal's position vis-à-vis its much larger neighbour India, which by itself has been regarded as a periphery of the industrialised West. Given that capitalism penetrated India at least a couple of centuries earlier than in Nepal with the beginning of British colonial rule, Nepal has been labelled as the periphery of the periphery that is India. Hence, when Indian nationalist leaders in the early twentieth century and even in the nineteenth century were going to the 'metropole' Britain for their higher education, Nepalese youths inspired by modern ideals at the time—most of whom belonged to the Hindu Bahun caste—were going to north Indian cities like Banaras for their education. Today, of course, Nepal has become a market for Indian goods, often goods made in India by well known western multinational companies. In this context, even the money earned by Nepalese working in India—from the Nepalese soldiers recruited in the Indian Army to the Nepalese working as guards and in restaurants in towns and cities across India—ultimately returns back to India as the money is spent in the consumption of Indian goods. (A recent phenomenon has been the influx of goods into Nepal from its other—and even larger—neighbour China. This has occasionally led to complaints from the Indian side about goods made in China entering the Indian market via Nepal.)

As the market creates its own economies of scale, along with making redundant traditional skills and knowledge systems, conventional ways of life become increasingly marginalised and ultimately disappear. They are unable to compete and survive in the capitalist world market. Given this, it is not surprising that the Nepalese perceive themselves as disadvantaged and exploited not only politically but also economically by their much larger neighbours like India. This is manifested in the saying popular among the hill Nepalese that a dead Indian (or a dead *Madhesi*, i.e. a person from the southern plains of Nepal) can fool a living Nepalese from the hills. The saying refers to the fact that the hill Nepalese do not have the appropriate new skills as well as the business acumen that the market has brought along with it, skills such as carpentry, masonry, electric-wiring, tailoring, plumbing or even hair cutting and business acumen like the running of retail shops and other such enterprises.

Unlike the Nepalese from the hills, Indians adept in the new skills and opportunities created by the market and with the required business acumen (not to mention the capital) have taken advantage of the openings provided by the market in Nepal, which by itself is becoming ever more integrated into the world capitalist economy. This has happened at the same time as the Nepalese are forced to work in unskilled employment not only in India but also in the Gulf countries, as well as elsewhere in the world. (Thus, as has been said, it is not brain drain from Nepal but "brawn drain," with Nepalese often involved in "three D" work, i.e. difficult, dirty and dangerous.)

The "inadequacy" among the Nepalese means that foreigners can find Nepal an attractive, as well as a lucrative, place for their skills. In this context, there finds mention of King Mahendra encouraging individuals from Darjeeling and Sikkim in India to come to Nepal and contribute in sectors like arts and literature. These individuals were supposed to contribute to the nation building project, i.e. the project of homogenisation around a so-called national language, culture and religion of the King-led Panchayat. There has also been mention of "Rangooniyas" chased from Myanmar coming to Nepal in the early 1960s. These Rangooniyas lent their "business acumen" and "entrepreneurial talent" to the traditional business houses and the political and bureaucratic power centres to initiate a dubious trade and exchange regime, thus destroying the traditional honesty existing in the Nepalese business community till then (Panday 2000: 408). The *Marwaris* from the deserts of Rajsthan in western India are yet another group to have come to Nepal to try their fortunes in the country. There abound anecdotes in the Nepalese society of the *Marwaris* coming to the country with only a jug (*lota*) and becoming millionaires through their trade and business practices. And with the sprouting of private "English" schools in the country from the 1980s, "convent-educated" youths from Darjeeling with their proficiency in the English language have found gainful employment in these private establishments. Another phenomenon related to the educational sector is the "Maths Science" teacher, i.e. teachers—this time not from India but from the southern plains of Nepal—with certificates from colleges and universities in north India to teach the "difficult" subjects of Mathematics and Science in government schools in the remote hill areas of the country. (There finds mention of the group of advisers of King Mahendra being replaced, following his death and the accession to the throne of his son Birendra, by "PhD Mafia" consisting of a group of well educated but relatively inexperienced young men upon whom Birendra depended for advice and guidance [Rose 1977: 237].)

All the new jobs that the market has created, from businesspersons and traders to skilled workers to educated professionals like teachers, doctors, engineers, etc. can be inaccessible to the vast majority of the Nepalese, including groups like the indigenous nationalities. Nepal is still largely a society where the money economy is a recent phenomenon, literacy is not universal and education—here I mean quality education with proficiency in the English language, computer skills and good command over one's subject matter—is a luxury. Hence, it is not surprising if many Nepalese perceive themselves as being "inadequate" vis-à-vis the rest of the world. It is a world that is alien where they have difficulty and feel discomfort adjusting to, let alone competing against. Also, it is a world that can expose their "inadequacy" in painfully embarrassing ways. An example in this regard is the difficulty that some Nepalese educated intellectuals have in taking their wives to urban parties. Their wives, whom they might have married before they became "urban" or even "intellectual" enough, can appear out of place in the urban milieu, given the way they dress, talk, partake of their food, etc. They are un-cool or, to use the more appropriate Khas-Nepali world in this context, they are simply "Pakhe."

As the market creates new skills, it also makes redundant old ones. And given modernity's emphasis on change for almost change's sake, we are forced to accept the new as also the good. The skills that might have made a vital contribution in a traditional economy come to be regarded as unproductive in the changed circumstances. Also, the accompanying ways of life are seen as useless, or even outright bad. The rural agrarian economy in Nepal has traditionally been one in which the entire family contributes. Thus, it is not surprising to see not only the grown-ups but also the young boys and girls contribute to the work in the household. These youths can fetch water, collect fodder for the cattle, collect wood for the fire and look after their smaller brothers and sisters. They can also contribute in the agricultural work, even digging or ploughing the fields, planting crops or weeding the crops. As the entire family is involved in the work, even small children may contribute to the household chores. These youths and children can do all this work and still go to school for "education" and—it has to be added, given the quality of education provided in government schools in the country—manage to do relatively well in their scholarly pursuits as well. The rural youths, one could say, are much more "mature," or they "mature" much earlier, than their urban counterparts.

In this context, an interesting observation has been made about the "new" phenomenon of the "teenager," not only in Nepal but also elsewhere in the world, for instance in North America. Until the middle of the nineteenth century, Americans noted no intermediate "adolescent" phase between childhood and adulthood. Children entered the work force at seven, with "full" incorporation for a male at around puberty. In Nepal, it has been said that just until a couple of decades ago there was no idea of this "middle group," i.e. the teenagers (Liechty 2008: 227). Today, of course, the situation is very much different, not only in Nepal but also all over the world, in places where modernity has made its mark. Teenagers have become a phenomenon, a social group by themselves in the modern world, often seen in a negative light as demanding, exasperating and even misbehaving. They can be contrasted with the young boys and girls in a traditional agrarian Nepalese society behaving responsively, working from an early age for the welfare of one's family and contributing productively to the household.

The way globalisation and its accompanying way of life impinges—and even negatively impacts—upon other ways of life, thus distorting and destroying it, becomes evident from the comments reported of a politician below. The politician, one of the top leaders of a communist party that, post-1990, has successfully participated in parliamentary politics, namely the Communist Party of Nepal (Unified Marxist-Leninist), was referring to the changed context in a changed world. The leader stated that those individuals who do not have phone in their home, television and sofa in their home and those who are not able to invite administrative and political persons to their home for even a cup of tea would find it difficult to become leaders of the party. The leader suggested that they should take time off from the party to arrange those things before becoming involved in the party again (Subedi 2004: 3). For a political party that had begun by cutting off the heads of "feudals" in the early 1970s, this was a grave and rather belated realization and must have come as a shock to many of the cadres of the party.

The Political Context

Politicians and political parties, not to mention intellectuals, writers and others, have of course played a not insignificant part in the modernising of the Nepalese society, or in bringing the fruits of modernity to the Nepalese society. In this regard, Nepalese politicians resemble the politicians of other developing countries around the world. These politicians, inspired by the meta or grand narratives of the early and mid-twentieth century like decolonisation, modernisation, nationalism and development, have tried to transform their respective societies accordingly. There has, in this context, been pointed to the attempt in a developing country like India of reconciling the political form, i.e. the liberal democratic state of a model of modernity, which is based upon features that were relatively weak in India, namely industrialisation, rationalism, the secularisation of society, individuation and democratization with the reality of India itself (Chiriyankandath 1999). The attempt was to develop a common civil identity, irrespective of religious or other differences. In this context, the mid-twentieth century Indian nationalist leader B.R. Ambedkar saw India wanting in its recognition of the principle of fraternity (Gupta 1998: 512). Ambedkar, who has appeared today as a messiah of the *dalit*, was scathing in his attack on village India as "a sink of localism, a den of ignorance, narrowmindedness and communalism" (Chiriyankandath 1999). Many non-Western developing societies, in the process of democratising themselves, thus face challenges unlike in the West, where the capitalist disciplining of a peasant work force through brutal production regimes, establishment of a secular state to avoid endless civil wars between religious groups vying for control of the state and the birth of a modern civil society, of individuation all preceded the beginning of the democratic process (Kaviraj 1996).

As in other developing countries, Nepalese politicians inspired by modern ideals have also provided their leadership in the political changes the country has undergone in the century past. They, too, inspired by modern nationalist ideals have sought to emphasise upon the fraternity or the solidarity of a common Nepalese people/nation. This has not always been an easy task, given the divisions within the Nepalese society and the accompanying inequalities based on these divisions. The making of the Nepalese state, which has been called by the ruling castes of the Nepalese society as the national unification of the country, was itself a particularly bloody affair. Groups like the indigenous nationalities resisted the encroachment by the Nepalese state, leading to confrontations and rebellions (see, for instance, Serchan 2007: 34-35). These groups have contested the process through which the Nepalese state destroyed their languages, cultures and ways of life to being labelled as national unification. They have come to refer to their present state of affairs as internal colonisation.

Although the three-decade long Panchayat constructed a nationalism revolving around one people/nation, one language, one culture, one religion and one dress, it failed to reduce the glaring inequalities in the Nepalese society. All the sectors of the Nepalese society, from the political to the administrative, from the academia to the civil society to the police and the army, continue to be dominated by the hill Hindu "high" caste groups, especially the Hindu Bahun. In the two hundred years of the country's history, all of its Prime Ministers barring one have come from the hill Hindu "high" caste groups. The lone exception was an individual from the Newar indigenous nationality group. The hill Hindu "high" castes have traditionally tended to regard themselves as the rulers and to look down upon the other groups of the Nepalese society as the ruled. When Sukraraj Shastri, one of the four martyrs of 1941, stated that he only wanted his rights, the Rana rulers of the time declared that in "our rule" what right of "you Newar," i.e. Sukraraj who belonged to the Newar indigenous nationality group (Gautam 1989/90: 183).

Nevertheless, the powerful ideology of the nation-state, nationalism and nation building that were sweeping the developing countries around the mid-twentieth century meant that groups like the indigenous nationalities were forced to forego their distinct identities and merge themselves into the Nepalese "nation." To be "national" or "nationalist" at the time meant being modern, progressive, forward looking, while the emphasising of one's ethnicity reflected a parochialism, a narrowmindedness unbecoming of the age. In this context, some even went to the extent of forsaking their ethnic/caste names and adopting the surname of 'Nepali.' Others gave up their ethnic/caste names and adopted in its place titles like *Kisan* (Farmer), *Prashrit* (Dependent), *Tuhure* (Orphan), *Rasik* (Romantic), *Byathit* (Sufferer), *Janglee* (Wild), *Anand* (Happiness), *Bhikshu* (Beggar), *Kamaro* (Slave), *Jwala* (Flame), etc.

Along with the metanarrative of nationalism, issues like political rights, social justice and economic prosperity have also predominated in the modernising process of the Nepalese state. The two other grand narratives of the twentieth century, namely democracy and communism have figured prominently in this process. The two metanarratives have come to symbolise in the Nepalese context political freedom and economic well-being sometimes seen as mutually exclusive of one another. The two narratives are perhaps best represented by the two political parties established around the middle of the twentieth century, viz. the Nepali Congress and the Nepal Communist Party. The two parties have continued to dominate the political scene in the country to this day, although the Nepal Communist Party over the years has split into over a dozen groups.

The first political party widely regarded as such to be established in the country is the *Praja Parishad* (literally, People's Council). The party established in 1936 aimed to free the Nepalese people from the oppressive family rule of the Ranas and to establish constitutional government in the country where every individual could enjoy to the fullest extent civil liberties and fundamental rights. The President of the party had apparently been influenced by the Enlightenment thinker Jean-Jacques Rousseau's book *The Social Contract.* In one of its pamphlets, the party stated that the law is simply a "contract" among the members of a society, hence no one but the society itself has the right to formulate it. A society that has not possessed this right cannot be called independent. The government, the party proclaimed, is an institution whose duty is to enforce the laws made by the society. Therefore, the government should be in accordance with the wishes of the society. The party declared that it had been established to make the Nepalese people among the civilised peoples of the world and to liberate the people by giving them proper education and to take the country forward in progress (see Serchan 2001: 37-38).

If the *Praja Parishad* aimed to take the country forward on the path of progress, the other political parties established in the country have also seen their mission to be of change and progress not only in the political but also in the social and cultural realms. At the time of the Nepali Congress-led "revolution" of 1950-51 that ended the 104-year old family rule of the Ranas, enthusiastic youths struck a blow against tradition by cutting the tuft of hair (*tupi*) kept on the head by the Hindu Brahman-Bahun. Along with the political "revolution" against the Ranas, there was also what has been called the Plough Revolution (*halo kranti*).

Given that the Brahman-Bahun have traditionally shunned physical labour of any kind, the hill Hindu Bahun did not plough their field by themselves, instead using hired labourers to do the work. Following the 1950-51 "revolution," youths belonging to the hill Hindu Bahun caste publicly undertook the ploughing of fields, thus breaking a social taboo. The Popular Movement of 1990 that ended the Panchayat and restored multiparty democracy in the country had not only political but also social and cultural overtones. This was manifested at the time in the declarations to make 'a New Nepal,' especially by the leaders and supporters of the Nepali Congress. The recent 2006 movement that ended the monarchy and made Nepal a republic, too, has come with its own social and cultural overtones, with the constant repetition once again of the phrase 'a New Nepal.'

Like the "social democratic" Nepali Congress, Nepalese communists, too, have conceived of the change and modernisation of the Nepalese society. Communists all over the world, from China to the Soviet Union, from Cuba to North Korea have after all dreamt of—and eagerly anticipated—the 'New Socialist/Communist Man' to come of the future. Given this, it is not surprising if Nepalese communists, like communists the world over, have railed against the old established order as "feudal," "bourgeois," seeking to displace and even destroy it. Nepalese communists have denounced the "bourgeois" way of life, "bourgeois" culture and "bourgeois" democracy. Some have even gone to the extent of forsaking the formal education provided in colleges and universities, labelling it as "bourgeois" education. Like the use of the word 'Citizen' to address one another, the commoner as well as the well-to-dos, following the French Revolution, the communists have popularised the word 'Comrade' in the Nepalese society. (The Nepali Congress, on the other hand, adopted the greeting "Jaya Nepal," literally meaning 'May Nepal Prosper,' in place of the traditional Hindu greeting of "Namaskar.")

The early 1970s saw the "campaign to eliminate class enemies" by some communists in the eastern tarai district of Jhapa. These young communists undertook a violent campaign, killing several persons they termed as "feudals," "landlords" and "class enemies." A "revolutionary" song of the time emphatically proclaimed that "without cutting the heads of feudals, without fighting against the army, New People's Democracy will not come just by begging for it" (INSEC 1997: 77-78). Of course, the most violent manifestation of radical communist ideology in the Nepalese context has been the recently concluded "people's war." The death toll from the decade-long war launched by the Unified Communist Party of Nepal (Maoist) crossed 13,000, not mentioning the countless others injured or maimed for life. The Maoists during their "people's war" not only aimed to establish a new political order (New People's Democracy, People's Republic, etc.) to replace the "old" multiparty parliamentary democracy, but also a new culture (New People's Democratic culture, etc.) to replace what they perceived as the old and rotten feudal and bourgeois culture and way of life.

In this context, the Maoists during their "people's war" were not only accused of killing and persecuting their political enemies, i.e. individuals belonging to political parties other than their own, but also of destroying and desecrating temples and other religious places, disallowing the performing of religious and cultural ceremonies in the villages and the killing and eating of cows. They undertook "New People's Democratic" marriages in place of traditional marriage ceremonies, built "Martyrs Gates" to commemorate their dead and came to mark, in place of traditional festivals and holidays, days—for instance the 1st of Falgun (February 13), i.e. the day when they had begun their "people's war"—as their own special days of celebration. The Maoists would no doubt claim that through their activities they were undertaking a revolution not only in the political but also in the social and cultural realms, displacing the old and ushering in the new, which was also concomitantly the good.

The tearing down of the old and replacing it by what they perceive as the new and the good by communists like the Maoists is not surprising, given that communism remains the most extreme as well as the most ambitious manifestation of the project of modernity. "Marxist revolutionism" represents one aspect of Enlightenment belief. Revolutionary socialism, i.e. communism has been one of the great projects of modernity, with its roots in the Enlightenment belief in the perfectibility of human affairs through reason and rational organisation (Sakwa 2002: 98).

To stand unequivocally for change, for "progress" has, therefore, characterised communists all over the world. In Nepal, the label applied to the communists of 'progressive'—similar to the one applied to the supporters and sympathisers of the Nepali Congress of 'democrat'—says it all. In this context, I can tell from my own experience that if you behave considerately to your subordinates, for instance if you carry your own bag and do not order your subordinates to do so, if you are willing to sit and eat on the same table with the *dalit*, you might well come to be regarded in the Nepalese society as a communist. (In a traditional "Hindu" society where the very touch of the "lowly" castes has been considered defiling, Nepalese communists are well known for their enthusiastic, even painful grip while shaking hands.)

The issues related to the various ethnicities, languages and cultures of the country are, however, much more complex. Nepalese communists have given some thought to and written about the issues of ethnicity (or nationality), language and of "oppressed" groups and minorities, and have in their documents raised their voices for a secular state, linguistic equality, ethnic and regional autonomy and even the right to self-determination. They no doubt had a significant role to play in making the country secular. All this can be contrasted with the major democratic party of the country, i.e. the Nepali Congress. Nonetheless, despite issues like ethnicity and language figuring in the documents of communist parties, their dissemination and propagation—acceptance is of course an entirely different thing, a bridge too far—among the wider Nepalese public has been another matter. This no doubt has to do with the prevailing powerful ideology of "nationalism."

After the Unified Communist Party of Nepal (Maoist) during its "people's war" in 2001 divided the country into nine autonomous regions, the party has come under attack from various quarters, including from fellow communists. The charges labelled against it range from "separatism" to "attempts to break up the country" to accusations of planting the "poison-tree" of ethnicity in the Nepalese society. The charges, in a nutshell, reflect the primacy that the ideology of "nationalism" has in our times. Anything seen as attacking the concept of the nation-state will invite negative comments not only from "rightists" but also from "leftists" like the communists. Nepalese communists, in spite of their internationalist pretensions, have sometimes appeared as the most strident advocates of the nationalist cause.

The sanctity and the inviolability of the concept of the nation-state is such that any deviation from its accepted symbols will provoke resentment. The Maoists, after entering into the government, parliament and the Constituent Assembly, have appeared in the "modern" dress of shirt and trousers. They have discarded the *daura suruwal* and *sari* that the Hindu Nepalese state has propagated as the "national" dress of the country. Women ministers belonging to the Maoists have worn shirt, jeans, trousers and jacket. (This despite the fact that the Maoists during their "people's war" had taken action against girls wearing jeans, trousers, along with other "fashionable" items.) After the Maoists came to head the government following elections to the Constituent Assembly, the Prime Minister appeared in a business suit complete with a tie, including in his trips to foreign countries. The modern continues to intrude upon what is still a traditional, even a conservative, Nepalese society in various ways, in various guises and in various forms, leading to ambivalence, anguish and even anger.

4

Multiculturalism and the Modern World

The years 1789-1989 beginning with the French Revolution and ending with the collapse of bureaucratic state socialism have been regarded as "the symbolic two centuries span of modernity" (Lyon 2002: 9). Today, a civilisational trajectory inaugurated by the Enlightenment has turned full circle and is now in its declining stages. The notion of transition as a logical phase in the development of society from a recognised starting point to a known end has its roots in the great metanarratives of modernity, of lineal and universal development patterns for all societies, which itself is derived from Christian thought. In this context, the trinity of the Enlightenment—reason, nature and progress—is said to have triumphed over and superseded the earlier (Christian) trinity (Ibid.: 10 and Sakwa 2002: 3).

Modernity's claims to universality have of course foundered against reality. Apart from the paradox of universalism I mentioned in the previous chapter, Enlightenment universality did not preclude the colonisation and the plunder and pillage of non-Western societies and its peoples by the West. Gender has been another blind spot in Enlightenment thinking, and it was only in the twentieth century that women were able to achieve 'universal' suffrage. In a country like Switzerland, which today has appeared as a model of the inclusive state, women achieved the right to vote only in 1971. Modernity can, therefore, be accused of being both 'imperial' and patriarchal, giving rise to racism as well as sexism.

And, despite the extravagant hopes of its *philosophes*, Enlightenment thinking has also foundered in its attempts to construct a rational morality. What we think of the good and bad, and also our convictions and beliefs regarding the good life remain beyond the range of mere logic (Schumpeter 1954: 251). There is no rational underpinning to morality, unless of course one takes refuge in pure instrumentality. Then many things in many different circumstances can become morally acceptable, or 'good.' Multiculturalism has come under attack not only from secular modernists but also religious conservatives, but there does not seem any way we can through rational argument and logic "evaluate" different cultures.

In this context, the only recourse seems to be to aspire towards a common minimum set of values that transcend cultural differences and can be acceptable to all of humanity. This is what Michael Walzer calls 'thin' and 'thick' morality (quoted in Huntington 1996: 318). This is what Jonathon Riley has called a 'two-tier structure' (Riley 2002: 82-83). Given that practical reason has proven incapable of "ranking" different cultures and settling the conflicts of values, individuals and groups are free to admire and choose their own social customs and practices as maximally suited to their own peculiar tastes. Cultures, therefore, are "thick," they prescribe institutions and patterns of behaviour to guide human beings in the paths which are considered right in a particular society. Nevertheless, there have to be at least some minimum set of human values for any way of life to be reasonably said to be to any degree moral, decent or true to our humanity. This is the "thin" minimal morality deriving from our common human condition, and can be said to be found in all cultures. These minimal moral concepts of truth and justice and common considerations of truth, morality and aesthetic taste are embodied in injunctions against murder, deceit, torture, enslavement, oppression and tyranny. They are also reflected in such vital interests that no one can possibly deny every human being in every society have, vital interests in subsistence, in not being attacked by others, in freedom from arbitrary arrest and enslavement, in freedom to emigrate and in at least some degree of freedom of conscience as well as freedom of thought and expression (Ibid.).

The "Paradigm" of Progress and Development

If reason remains incapable of providing a justification for morality, the Enlightenment belief in progress is just that, a belief. Even leaving aside the issue of the difficulty of evaluating cultures and societies across time, similar to that across space, there is no guarantee that tomorrow will be "better" than today, the day after tomorrow "better" than tomorrow and so on. The idea of progress bequeathed to us by the Enlightenment remains flawed. As Gurpreet Mahajan asks rhetorically, "Progress? All the generations that have passed away, merely for the last? Every individual, only for the species, that is for the image of the abstract name?" (Mahajan 1999).

Time is not only a road of course, it is also a room. We can think and act only within our own context, we are all children of our own particular time and place. In this context, instead of the concept of "progress," I think, "paradigm" might be more useful to us in our analysis here. I am of course using "paradigm" in the sense made famous by Thomas S. Kuhn in his book *The Structure of Scientific Revolutions*. Kuhn (1996) was referring to the way science is practiced. Paradigm refers to the accepted 'mode' or 'model' or 'pattern' of analysis that some particular scientific community acknowledges for the time being as supplying the foundation for its further practice. Every particular scientific discipline at a given time has "a set of recurrent and quasi-standard illustrations of various theories in their conceptual, observational and instrumental applications. These are the community's paradigms, revealed in its textbooks, lectures and laboratory exercises." They provide the framework to carry out further research in the field, they imply some shared values among the community. One can, thus, refer to the "Copernican paradigm" in astronomy, "Newtonian paradigm" in physics or the "Darwinian paradigm" in biology.

Paradigms achieve their status because "they are more successful than their competitors in solving a few problems that the groups of practitioners have come to recognise as acute." The new paradigm "implies a new and more rigid definition of the field." The old paradigm that it has replaced has become incapable of solving the acute problems, or "anomalies," that have appeared in the field. Thus, the concerned field of science, with the appearance of the new paradigm, undergoes a "revolution," a "paradigm shift." One can, in this context, point to the "Copernican paradigm" that replaced the old "Ptolemaic paradigm" in astronomy.

Until the existing paradigm is replaced by a new one, scientists continue to practice what Thomas S. Kuhn has called "normal science." They engage in "mopping up" or "puzzle-solving." All these are activities that reinforce the existing paradigm without bringing a fundamental change in its underlying structure. The latter occurs only with the advent of a new paradigm. Kuhn calls the scientists engaged in these "normal science" activities as "addicts," even comparing them derisively with the brainwashed characters of George Orwell's novel of communist dystopia *Nineteen Eighty-Four.*

As a philosopher of science, Thomas S. Kuhn was using paradigm to refer to the "hard" sciences, i.e. the natural sciences. But it remains applicable also with regard to the social sciences, not to mention the everyday affairs of life. Our everyday life continues to be molded by norms and values, ideas and ideals of the time and place we happen to live in. They guide us in the choices we make, choices not only related to practical life but also moral choices. Thus, what we regard as 'progress' and 'development' in a particular time may not be so in another period. Development may well turn out to be destruction in the long run. The mid-twentieth century had been the period of "nation building," and with the urge to build a strong nation-state the Nepalese state, too, had undertaken grandiose "national" gestures that extended the control of the centre all over the country. The nationalisation of forests by the elected Nepali Congress government in 1960, forests that had largely been under the control of groups like the indigenous nationalities, the centralisation of education in 1971 that detached education from the community and deprived education of effective community management and support, and the over-centralisation of the health system are some instances of this nation building project. Today, of course, the wheel has turned full circle, with the *Nepal Human Development Report 2001* pointing out that over-centralisation had been the bane of the country, and it had hindered "development" over the years. The Report stressed upon the community approach to the management of forests, community health schemes as well as pre-1971 community managed education systems (UNDP 2002).

The seductiveness of development is such that countries like Nepal continue to rush headlong towards it. This is despite the mention by some of "development fatigue" in the "developed" parts of the world (Giddens 1990). We all continue to be development "addicts." In this context, it is not surprising if Nepalese have been willing to destroy their fertile rice-growing fields to construct roads. Given that road remains among the most tangible, as well as one of the most easily quantifiable, manifestation of the so-called development, road building remains a high priority in government planning. This is matched and reciprocated by the zeal and enthusiasm among the people at large. There occur serious disputes among locals regarding the issue of a road that has been proposed to be built passing through one particular locality at the expense of another. Everybody wants the road to pass through their locality, or even better still, right in front of their household.

The "paradigm" of progress and development would have us believe in their inevitability, and also in that there are no limits to progress and development. It would have that the issues of progress and development take precedence over all the other issues in the society. All this can even lead to the patently absurd notion that the issues of progress and development are somehow culturally neutral. This is obviously not so. It is only that as some disciplines like economics, behind a façade of "instrumentality" and "rationality," are just better at hiding their cultural leanings (Smith 2002: 2), progress and development, too, can be made to appear to be neutral of cultural specificities. This is what some Nepalese politicians are attempting to do when they say that the federal division of the country should be on the basis of "development."

Given that one of the most—if not the most—complex issues facing the Constituent Assembly elected for drafting a new constitution is the 'implementation' of federalism, there have been put forth various proposals with regard to it. Politicians belonging to the ruling hill Hindu "high" castes Bahun and Chhetri have proposed that "development" be the basis for the federal division of the country. This is in opposition to proposals by groups like the indigenous nationalities, who want the country to be divided federally on the basis of ethnicity, language and region. A federal division of the country on a non-sociocultural basis, for instance on the basis of "development," would mean giving continuity to the one language, one culture policy of the Nepalese state of the last two centuries and more. A division along sociocultural lines, on the other hand, would mean the end of this hegemony, with the ruling castes of Bahun and Chhetri becoming "minorities," even the "ruled" in various parts of the country. (Of course, the rulers in the Nepalese society would not have acceded to the demands for federalism itself if it had not been for the *Madesh* movement in early 2007. The movement forced the rulers to capitulate and include, through an amendment, 'federalism' in the Interim Constitution of Nepal 2007.) In this context, one could say that the ruling groups of the Nepalese society aim to counter the increasing assertiveness among groups like the indigenous nationalities regarding their own culture, language and way of life with the enticement of the so-called development.

Development itself is of course inextricably bound up with politics, besides having social and cultural implications. During the Panchayat system the Nepalese state had sought to impose and legitimate a hegemonic Hindu "national" culture by homogenising the ethnically, culturally, linguistically and religiously diverse population of the country. A key to the legitimisation of the Panchayat rule was the doctrine of *bikas* or "development" as the national project (Tamang 2002: 161-163). Given that the Panchayat elite's need to legitimise itself coincided with the post-World War II global project of international development, it led to massive injections of foreign aid and assistance into Nepal. In this context, the project of development compounded the structured inequalities related to class and ethnicity in the Nepalese society, along with obliterating the heterogeneity of the varied peoples' lived experiences. All the diverse peoples of the country came to be defined as 'Nepali.' This included the creation of the "patriarchally oppressed, uniformly disadvantaged and Hindu 'Nepali woman'" (Ibid.).

The demise of the Panchayat in 1990 has not in any way stemmed the development tide. In fact, the governments of the post-1990 dispensation have competed against each other and have taken pride in the fact that they have been able to bring more foreign assistance for the country's "development." A novel feature following 1990, however, has been the influx of foreign assistance through non-governmental organisations—development through the "grassroots," or is it conquest from below? As non-governmental organisations have sprouted like "mushrooms" in the country after 1990, foreign donors have been able to channelise their assistance not only through the state but also through these organisations.

The non-governmental phenomenon has been such that an educated Nepalese looking to make a living post-1990 might well fancy his or her best chances to be in an international non-governmental organisation or in a local non-governmental organisation, or even in opening a non-governmental organisation by himself or herself. This present state of affairs can be compared with the 1980s when private "English" schools were an attractive option for employment. The educated of the time sought employment in these schools or, even better still, opened one themselves, either in the capital Kathmandu or in one of the towns around the country. (We certainly have come a long way from the days when the government was the most attractive, not to mention the sole, source of employment for the educated young Nepalese.)

Non-governmental organisations, be they engaged in 'service delivery,' 'advocacy' or in 'pure research,' have ushered in their own dynamics in the Nepalese society. Along with the fees of foreign consultants and development staff, as well as their local counterparts, one can in this context point to the never-ending circuit of seminars, workshops and conferences in star hotels, amidst sumptuous lunches and dinners, not to mention cocktail parties. There is also the hullabaloo over report writing, progress reports and "evaluation," "feasibility studies" and "pre-feasibility studies," "literature" that gather dust in some corner of the concerned offices virtually unread. All this, it is not too hard to say, is more for the benefit of the "providers" of development themselves, i.e. the consultants, staff, etc. involved than for its "recipients," i.e. the hapless common folks. The so-called development has spawned its own "development industry," as well as its own "development bureaucracy."

The common folks, who are supposed to be the recipients of development, become rather the "victims" of development. Not only do they have to endure lectures on "development" from those who are considered far more knowledgeable than they themselves regarding their own affairs, but they also have to provide their time and occasionally free labour to "development." The latter can be compared with the practice of the predatory Nepalese state of the past of extracting unpaid labour (*jhara*) from the common peoples for various activities.* As development imposes its own uniformity, the common folks have to

* As a researcher myself, one thing in particular that I have never been able to fathom is the morality of undertaking research by obtaining primary data from local peoples. Primary data implies observations, interviews, questionnaires, among other things. All this means taking the valuable time of local peoples. Even the act of observation means impacting upon and unsettling—to one extent or the other—the established rhythms of local lives. For all their troubles the locals get almost nothing in return. After all, pure research means that the locals are denied even the gestures of the so-called development. On the other hand, the researchers, through their research, are able to advance their professional careers, obtain tenures in prestigious universities, in short benefit financially as well as in other ways. Of course, it may be that given that it is the dominant group who determine what is good and what is not, i.e. the norms and values in any given society and as researchers, academics and intellectuals are among this dominant group, their actions remain beyond the purview of any ordinary morality. The question of ethics or morality simply does not arise in their own case.

obey and follow the dictates of the development agencies. They also have to fulfill the conditions and conditionalities laid out by such agencies. One common theme that can be observed in this regard, which also gets reported in newspapers, is the construction by the rural folks under the directives of non-governmental organisations of toilets (in reality pit latrines). The disposal of bodily waste has become a particular concern for development practitioners. (It also is apparently a global concern, as is indicated by the establishment of the WTO—not the World Trade Organization but the World Toilet Organization.)

As globalisation continues apace, it encroaches upon spaces that a particularly group or society may consider sacrosanct, even sacred. An observer, in this context, has pointed to the "curious phenomenon" in the contemporary world—the ever increasing homogenisation of humankind and the resistance to that homogenisation (Fukuyama 1992: 244). But there is obviously no contradiction here, if one realises that universalisation means uniformity. The "global citizen" or the "planetary citizen" envisioned by "globalists" would perhaps speak only one language and follow one culture and one way of life. They would wear the same dress, eat the same kind of food and observe the same routine in their daily lives. They would thus become truly universal, divested of all their particularities. (As the multinational company Pepsi's proud assertion puts it aptly—'one quality worldwide.')

In this context, many in the West would no doubt see a "civilisational highway" beginning in Mesopotamia and continuing through Egypt and the Middle East and passing through Greece and Rome to reach Europe and finally the United States, i.e. the West. They would also no doubt like to think that with globalisation the entire world and its peoples are ultimately benefitting from the fruits of this "civilisation." They would also perhaps wish to think that the West, and the modernity and the particular way of life it has engendered, somehow reflect and express "the essence of our species." Hegemonic Hindu discourse in Nepal, and in South Asia, would like to see the entire South Asia as their exclusive domain (*Akhand Bharat*), with everyone and everything within it becoming "Hindu." Assimilation and homogenisation, if not much worse, then become the tools to achieve their ends.

Hegemonic and homogenising discourses in Nepal and beyond ignore the reality—as well as the importance—of the varied ways of life of peoples around the world. They would also no doubt like to ignore such facts as that many of the presently existing 5000-6000 languages in the world are predicted to become extinct by the end of the twenty-first century. Groups like the indigenous nationalities, on the other hand, are affirming the "life-worlds" of diverse peoples around the world, people who have been marginalised by the so-called world histories, world religions and world civilisations.

The contribution of indigenous and tribal peoples to the cultures and achievements of the world has not been insignificant, although it has not always been recognised and acknowledged. The declaration by the United Nations of the International Day of the World's Indigenous Peoples and the International Decade of the World's Indigenous Peoples and the setting up of the United Nations Permanent Forum on Indigenous Issues are belated recognition and acknowledgement of this. The Department of Public Information of the United Nations states that many of the world's staple foods like peepers, potatoes, lentils, peas, sugarcane, garlic and tomatoes were first cultivated by indigenous peoples. There are many words in the English language like canoe, barbeque, squash, powwow and moccasin that are derived from the various indigenous languages of the Americas. Also, around seventy-five percent of the world's plant-based pharmaceuticals, including aspirin, digitalis and quinine, have been derived from medicinal plants found in tribal areas, with most of the 7,000 natural compounds used in modern medicine having been employed by traditional healers for centuries.

The Indigenous Nationality Revival

The indigenous and "tribal" peoples of Nepal have, following the political change of 1990, not only named themselves as indigenous nationalities (*Adibasi Janajati* in Khas-Nepali), but have also defined what they mean by indigenous nationalities. They have also identified the groups in the Nepalese society who are indigenous nationalities.

By identifying themselves as *Adibasi Janajati*, the Nepalese indigenous nationalities have struck at the hegemonic Hindu discourse of the past two centuries and more. By identifying themselves as *Janajati*, they are, directly or indirectly, affirming that they are not Hindus. And by identifying themselves as *Adibasi*, they have raised their voices on behalf of the 'first settlers' of the country. A notable feature of the making of the Nepalese state has been that the Nepalese rulers, from the Shah kings to the Rana oligarchs, have claimed their ancestry to the south, namely to 'Hindu' India. Although the Nepalese kings and rulers may be descended from indigenous nationality groups native to the country like the Magar, they have attempted to embellish their genealogies with references to the south. Hence, the recently deposed Shah dynasty and the Shah kings are said to be the descendents of the Rajput 'Sisodiya clan' of Chittor in India. They apparently came to Nepal fleeing the Islamic onslaught in the south around the thirteenth century. This attempt to trace one's roots to the south has meant that 'Hinduisation' or 'Sanskrisation' has been the norm during Nepal's state-making process. It has also meant that the natives of the country, i.e. the indigenous nationalities have come to be denigrated and looked down upon as inferior, even as second class citizens in their own lands during the making of the Nepalese state (Kumar 2000: 44).

Today, by emphasising upon their indigenous-ness, Nepalese indigenous nationalities have challenged established and long-accepted discourses. By emphasising upon their own language, culture and way of life, they have struck at the monolithic nationalism constructed by the Nepalese state. The Nepalese indigenous nationalities through their activities are affirming the multicultural reality of the Nepalese society, something that the Nepalese state had ignored and repudiated. Their actions are best understood not only in the context of a homogenising Nepalese state, but also within the wider globalising world.

Among the major demands of the Nepalese indigenous nationalities are secular state, equality of languages, affirmative action, federalism, ethnic autonomy, right to self-determination and the right to their land and natural resources. If these are some of the issues of the indigenous nationalities that are directly related to the Nepalese state, the issues nonetheless also have a larger context. Nepalese indigenous nationalities have drawn inspiration from the two international instruments directly related to indigenous peoples, namely the International Labour Organisation Convention No. 169 on Indigenous and Tribal Peoples and the United Nations Declaration on the Rights of Indigenous Peoples. They have also found inspiration and solidarity with the worldwide movement of indigenous peoples and have participated in various international fora of indigenous peoples, including in the United Nations Permanent Forum on Indigenous Issues.

The Nepalese state, in the context of the increasing assertiveness among indigenous nationalities, has brought forth some measures to address their demands. These include affirmative action and reservation for marginalised groups like the indigenous nationalities. They also include the establishment of the National Foundation for Development of Indigenous Nationalities. The demand of indigenous nationalities for a secular state has been heeded by making Nepal secular following the Popular Movement of 2006. Also, the Nepalese state has been forced to accede to the demand for federalism following the *Madhes* movement. Today, after the formation of an elected Constituent Assembly to draft a new constitution, the agenda of the restructuring of the Nepalese state has been put at the forefront of the Nepalese society. Nepalese indigenous nationalities hope that their demands like equality of languages, ethnic autonomy or ethnic federalism and the right to their traditional lands and natural resources will be incorporated in the new constitution to be made by the Constituent Assembly.

The demands of Nepalese indigenous nationalities, like that of indigenous peoples around the world, reflect their concern over their languages, cultures and ways of life in the face of increasing uniformity and homogenisation. These concerns and worries, even fears, vis-à-vis their identity and their recognition by the wider world are the motivating factors behind the movements of indigenous peoples, along with that of other sociocultural groups around the world. These worldwide movements strike at the two metanarratives of modernity, namely nationalism or the nation-state and universalism or globalisation.

Nepalese indigenous nationalities have demanded that the decennial censuses undertaken by the Nepalese state enumerate their ethnic, linguistic and religious identities distinctly and appropriately. This was a particular concern at the time of the last census in 2001, and will no doubt also be an issue at the time of the next census in 2011. The indigenous nationalities have called for the retention of the original names in the indigenous nationality languages of the villages, hills, mountains, rivers, lakes, caves, etc. The Nepalese state, in the process of Hinduisation, had even gone to the extent of changing the original names of these places, renaming them in the language of the ruling Hindu castes, i.e. Khas-Nepali. The indigenous nationalities have demanded that the original names of such places be restored. They have also, expressing concern over their distinct identities, urged their fellow indigenous nationalities to name their children in their own languages.

The concerns over culture can, not surprisingly in today's world, take on a typically postmodern twist, with culture not to be lived but to be shown and seen and observed. This is manifested in the establishment of 'Ethnographic Museum' and in concepts like ethno-tourism and cultural tourism. It also finds manifestation in 'cultural festivals,' 'food festivals' and in documentaries, films and the like. All these are expressions of culture as something to be shown and seen, culture as exhibition so to say.

Nevertheless, the expression of pride in one's culture is in marked contrast to the past. The process of Hinduisation or Sanskritisation imposed by the Nepalese state had led in the past not only to introversion but also to a feeling of inferiority among the indigenous nationalities. This happened with the Hindu Nepalese state making the Hindu religion, culture and way of life as the 'standard' in the Nepalese society, while negating, stereotyping and marginalising all other cultures and ways of life. Given this, it is not entirely surprising if indigenous nationality groups in the past had attempted to undertake various measures to "reform" their particular societies. The indigenous nationality group Magar in the 1950s established the 'Association for the Reform of Magar Society.' The aim of the Society was not only to unify the Magars but also to eliminate their "bad customs" (Lecomte-Tilouine 2004: 113). (The use of the word 'Reform' in the name of the Society is of course significant). Another indigenous nationality group the Tharu of the tarai undertook special "social reform" movements within their society proscribing, among other things, the drinking of alcohol, eating of pig and the raising of poultry, and disallowing their womenfolk to move freely, smoke and chew betels and to enter into the kitchen or cook meals during the menstrual period (Srivastava 1999: 20).

If in the past indigenous nationalities had attempted to "reform" their society with the aim of Hinduising or Sanskritising it, the situation at present is different. Today's 'politics of recognition' stresses pride in one's own identity, in one's own culture and way of life. This is not to say that groups like the indigenous nationalities are totally free to act in ways unencumbered by the time and place they happen to be in. Like the rural folks 'forced' by non-governmental organisations to make pit latrines in their homes, despite their objections that such toilets are "smelly," the indigenous nationality groups also have their own constraints to deal with. As the society's "paradigm" changes, so do norms and values and the way of looking at things, with even "truths" being in and out of favour according to the times. In this context, indigenous nationality groups like the Gurung and Magar may be feeling bemused at the fact that their traditional youth association of the *Rodhi* had in the past come under censure for promoting sexual laxity and immorality. Today, of course, the celebrating of 'Valentine's Day' has become an annual ritual among "modern" urban youths, with even the practice of 'dating' not being uncommon in metropolises like Kathmandu.

Writing Themselves

A feature of the modern society is that it is a 'written' society, along with being a money economy. The emphasis on the written over the oral is despite the fact that so much of the human experience is 'unwritten,' it never gets documented and never will be. The written in our times has unequivocal precedence over the merely oral. Hence, it is only the written histories of the West that come to be regarded as 'true' histories, while the histories of other societies become "myths." The materials on which these supposedly true histories are based show their bias towards the written. Thus, in a society that is still not today a fully monetised economy like the Nepalese society, histories nonetheless come to be based on the finds of 'coins' that some king or the other had supposedly promulgated in the centuries past. These written histories disregard the past and tradition and the knowledge associated with such past and tradition that continues to live on in folk cultures, folk songs, folk dances, folk rituals as well as in sayings, proverbs, etc.

The emphasis on the written means that the oral is seen as a "lack," as being "inadequate" or "backward." In this context, newspapers have often reported about the "cave-dwelling" indigenous nationality group the Chepang not having citizenship certificates. The implication is that their not having such certificate reflects some kind of inadequacy, even a disability on the part of the Chepang. Given the precedence the written has over the oral in our times, groups like the Nepalese indigenous nationalities have not surprisingly taken steps towards "writing" their languages, cultures and ways of life.

Like the Chepang today eager to obtain citizenship certificate from the concerned Nepalese government authorities, indigenous nationalities have shown their enthusiasm in documenting themselves. An example of this are the dictionaries that have been brought forth of various indigenous nationality languages. As language remains one of the most tangible manifestations of a culture, the preservation of their language is of particular concern to groups like the indigenous nationalities. The speaking of one's own language, the passing down of one's language to one's children and the teaching of one's own language have become a particular concern among the indigenous nationalities. With this aim in mind, indigenous nationalities have undertaken steps towards the standardisation of their languages through dictionaries. They have also brought forth textbooks and other materials for the teaching of their languages. (The "anxiety" vis-à-vis the written can be seen from the occasional comments of indigenous nationalities that their written scripts have been "lost" or "destroyed." It would of course be more correct to say that as oral societies the various indigenous nationality groups never had scripts in the past.)

The attempts by indigenous nationalities at preserving their cultures by "writing" them or documenting them are steps they have taken towards being modern, being up-to-date with the times. Nepal is still not a society well known for maintaining records and documenting things in the way of the modern industrialised societies of the West. This "inadequacy" has manifested itself in various fields. An example that could be cited in this regard is that of citizenship certificates. There have been accusations that an "Indian" managed to become not only a member of the Constituent Assembly elected in 2008, but also became a minister in the Nepalese government formed after the elections! Given the "inadequacy" in maintaining records and documenting things in the traditional Nepalese society, the above-mentioned "Indian," one way or the other, apparently managed to acquire Nepalese citizenship certificate, thus becoming a *bona fide* Nepalese citizen and even going on to hold a top government post.

The enthusiasm for "writing" themselves among groups like the indigenous nationalities has given rise to its own dynamic, its own consequences. The standardisation of language through the publication of dictionaries, the bringing forth of textbooks and other teaching materials and the documenting and writing of histories are all the consequences of being a written society. Like the Khas-Nepali speaking Hindu Nepalese state that has brought forth its "pioneer poet" (a Hindu Bahun writing in the Khas-Nepali language) and "national poet" (another

Hindu Bahun writing in the Khas-Nepali language), various indigenous nationality groups have also brought forward their pioneer poet/national poet in their respective languages. The creating and the writing of their own "national" icons will no doubt continue, indeed gather momentum, as the indigenous nationality groups progress further on the path towards becoming a "written," a modern society. (The concept of the nation is something that I will explore further in the next chapter.)

If groups like the indigenous nationalities have struck at the two grand narratives of modernity, viz. the nation-state and universalisation, while at the same time aspiring to be modern in so many other ways, their ambivalence vis-à-vis the idea of progress and development is also not entirely unexpected. The "ideology" of development is so powerful in societies like ours—societies considered as poor, backward or, more politically correctly, as developing—that to speak against such development can be tantamount almost to treason. The phrase *bikas-birodhi* in Khas-Nepali (i.e. those who oppose development) remains among the most damning abuses that can be hurled against anyone in the present Nepalese society. This is why land speculation, i.e. not only the buying and selling of land but also its "plotting" to build apartment blocks and housing colonies in urban centres, including in the traditional areas of indigenous nationalities, has become such a thriving business. It is why a farmer who in the past might have worked on the land today prefers to build a house on the land so that he or she can sit back and earn the rent—"rent-seeking" literally—by letting out the house.

Nevertheless, Nepalese indigenous nationalities through their actions have come to question the discourse of development. Concepts like "free, prior and informed consent" put forth in international instruments have also come to figure in the discourse of Nepalese indigenous nationalities. This is especially in relation to their ancestral lands and the natural resources lying therein. The encroachment upon and the appropriation and confiscation of the lands and natural resources of indigenous nationalities have been a feature of the making of the Nepalese state. This has found continuation in the name of modern development programs and projects and in policies of the state like "resettlement" and "land reforms." Today, indigenous nationalities are stating that any activity in their lands has to be with their free, prior and informed as well as willingly given consent.

The questioning of the so-called development by indigenous nationalities can perhaps be illustrated with an example from Kathmandu, the capital of Nepal and also the traditional homeland of the indigenous nationality group the Newar, and the project that has been associated with it for the last couple of decades, namely the Melamchi Water Supply Project. The Melamchi Project is supposed to provide drinking water to the parched Kathmandu-ites by bringing water through a 27 k.m.-long tunnel from a river to the north beyond the Kathmandu Valley. Given the acute shortage of water in the Valley due to the explosion in population during the last couple of decades, politicians have often pointed to the Melamchi Project as the panacea to the water woes of Kathmandu Valley.

As a "development" project, the Melamchi Project is not uncontroversial, although not untypically there has been the tendency to sweep these controversies under the carpet in the name of development by the politicians, development planners and bureaucrats in the capital Kathmandu. The place and the river from where water is to be brought for the Melamchi Project is the traditional homeland of another indigenous nationality group, i.e. the Hyolmo. The name of the project, namely the Melamchi Water Supply Project does not recognise this, given that 'Melamchi' is neither the name of the place nor the name of the river from where the water is to be brought.

Even more importantly, water is hardly the abundant resource that it is sometimes made out to be in Nepal. It appears so primarily because it has yet to be tapped to the fullest extent possible as in modern societies. Not only are hydroelectric projects on rivers not that common in the country, with load-shedding in urban centres like Kathmandu being the norm, but everyday water usage is also hardly at the optimum that it could be as in "developed" modern societies. There are still large tracts of agricultural land in the country that do not have access to irrigation and have to rely on monsoon rains for water-intensive crops. Also, many households in the country do not have access to piped or running water in their homes. Even where homes have been connected with water pipes, the water supply can be highly irregular, as is the case with Kathmandu. Indeed, it is precisely because of the severe water shortage in Kathmandu that politicians have for years been able to sell the "dream" of Melamchi to the parched Kathmandu Valley denizens.

When talking about the utilisation of such an important resource as water, there are issues related to both quantity as well as quality. As societies become "modern" and "developed," the tapping into nature to fulfill human need, even human greed, increases exponentially. A traditional society can literally live off the land, with a way of life that is in marked contrast to modern societies. A foreign observer has pointed to the lack of cleanliness and sanitation and unhygienic conditions that existed in the towns of the Kathmandu Valley in the late nineteenth century (Daniel Wright, quoted in Gurung 2001: 128). The situation was such that there used to be outbreaks of cholera every couple of years or so. Today, the people are not only more health conscious, but standards of cleanliness have also improved. This will no doubt continue in the future as well, as the Nepalese society becomes more and more "modern." All this means the use of water, to keep not only one's surroundings clean but also to keep oneself clean (for instance, by taking a bath at least once a day).

In this context, indigenous nationality groups like the Hyolmo may in the future come to regret "providing" such a vital natural resource as water to Kathmandu through the Melamchi Project. Given the "doctrine of prior use," they may not be able to do anything about the decision in the future. They may well feel they were "bulldozed" into the decision without their "free, prior and informed consent." With regard to the indigenes of Kathmandu, i.e. the Newar, the bowl-shaped structure of the Kathmandu Valley means that today's "development," with its location as the capital of the country, its urban sprawl, overcrowding, pollution, etc. may well turn out to be an environmental disaster of the future, not to mention the consequences for the culture and way of life of the Newar. An organisation of the Newar, namely the *Newa Deya Dabu* (Newar National Forum), in this context, has called for the proposed "outer" Ring Road in the Kathmandu Valley to be built only following consultation with the Newar themselves. (The proposed "outer" Ring Road will encircle the currently existing "inner" Ring Road.)

The questioning of the idea of progress and development by Nepalese indigenous nationalities, their claims to their lands and natural resources, their calls for ethnic autonomy/federalism have consequences for the future of the Nepalese state, as well as for the type of political system it adopts. Not only the modern metanarrative of nationalism but also of liberal democracy do not remain unchallenged in this context. The actions of the indigenous nationalities call into question these grand narratives of modernity. In the next chapter, I attempt to explore these issues, taking into account not only the Nepalese context but also the broader global context.

5

Democracy, the Nation-State and a Multicultural World

A western political scientist who had written of the universalisation of western liberal democracy as the final form of human government was to later state that the ethnic conflicts and immigrant movements around the world in recent years have revealed a sizeable hole in the traditional liberal political theory. By treating citizens only as individuals, the liberal state ignores the group-oriented character of real-world populations that, for better or worse, find great satisfaction in ascriptive collective identities (Fukuyama 1992: 4 and 1996: 323).

Liberalism takes the individual as the ultimate and irreducible unit of society and explains the latter in terms of it, and is thus individualist and finds it difficult to offer a coherent account of the community. Liberalism determines the nature of the state (formal, abstract), its structure (separate from the autonomous civil society, a clear separation between public and private), its rationale (protection of the basic rights of its citizens) and its basic limits (individuals rather than groups or communities) (Parekh 1993: 157-165). The liberal conviction that there are certain inviolable private and individual rights raises decisive barriers to what the *demos* may decide for the common good (O'Donnel 1998: 113-114). Liberalism, it has been stated, is an inspiring political doctrine stressing such great values as human dignity, autonomy, liberty, critical thought and equality. Nevertheless, these values can be defined in several different ways, of which the liberal is only one and not always the most coherent. Liberalism also ignores or marginalises such other great values as human solidarity, community, a sense of rootedness, selflessness, deep and self-effacing humility and contentment. Given that it grasps only some aspects of the immensely complex human existence and misses out too much of what gives value to life, liberalism, or socialism or for that matter any other political doctrine, cannot provide the sole basis of the good society (Parekh 1999).

The attacks that liberalism and Western liberal democracy has had to face in recent years have led one non-Western observer to comment that the failure of Marxism, one of the great projects of modernity, and the dramatic break-up of the Soviet Union are only the precursors to the collapse of Western liberalism, the main current of modernity. Far from being the alternative to Marxism and the reigning ideology at the end of history, liberalism will be the next domino to fall (Takeshi Umehara, quoted in Huntington 1996: 306). The collapse of the Soviet Union, in this context, is likely to appear as the prelude to an epoch of Western decline. The ruin of Soviet Marxism was, after all, the failure of an universalist Western ideology, of a species of the Enlightenment project. It was not the end but the resumption of history, in forms as little likely to be liberal as they are to be ever again Marxist (Gray 1998: 96). Thus, the fall of Soviet communism is most likely to occur as an incident in the decline of the Western cultures that gave it birth, as those cultures are shaken by the Malthusian ethnic and fundamentalist conflicts which—far more than any European ideology—seem set to dominate the twenty-first century (Ibid.). The "crises" faced by liberalism today can perhaps be gauged from the fact that the United Nations Development Programme in its annual Human Development Report series focused in the year 2004 on the theme of 'Cultural Liberty in Today's Diverse World.' The 2004 Report with contributions from such well known liberal thinkers like Amartya Sen and Will Kymlicka advocated an approach respecting and promoting cultural diversity primarily from a liberal perspective.

Democracy in Nepal

Despite the worldwide attacks on it, to talk of a "crisis" of democracy in the Nepalese context would perhaps be rather incongruous. This is in spite of the country being labelled "poor," "backward" or "developing." Democracy has indeed and truly been one of the metanarratives of twentieth century Nepalese society. If one looks back at twentieth century Nepalese history, one can see the aspirations for democracy among the educated middle classes of the country (see, for instance, Serchan 2001: Chapter 2). And by democracy here I mean democracy that goes beyond the merely "minimalist" definition of it, i.e. that of participation and contestation. A "minimalist democracy" implies the right as well as the ability of the people to replace, through the ballot, one set of rulers with another.

There is no doubting the importance of the citizens' right to change their rulers, rulers who may regard themselves as irreplaceable as well as immovable. By using this right the citizens can protect themselves from oppressive rule and tyranny. Nonetheless, the democratic discourse in Nepal has consistently gone beyond the "minimalist" definition of democracy. Modern democratic Nepalese constitutions have not only enshrined under fundamental rights such rights as the right to association and the right to form political parties, but also such rights as the freedom of conscience, of speech, of expression, of press and publication, among others. Although these rights are obviously not absolute, with restrictions on activities impinging upon "national" sovereignty and integrity, the "harmonious" relationship subsisting among various groups, activities contrary to decent public behaviour or morality, etc., there is no doubting the liberal inclination underlying these rights. Nepalese democracy as well as democratic aspirants have found inspiration and sought sustenance from, in principle if not always in practice, Western liberal democratic ideals.

The ideal of democracy has continued to inspire and guide educated Nepalese youths, although democracy as a political system in the Nepalese society *per se* has not gone unchallenged during the course of the century gone by. The Panchayat, an attempt at guided democracy with the all-powerful monarch assuming the guardianship of the polity, ended through a royal coup Nepal's first experimentation with democracy of the 1950s. The King-led Panchayat, though having to maintain the façade of democracy ("Panchayat Democracy"), emphasised upon the two other grand narratives of the Nepalese society, nationalism and development. The Panchayat, with regard to development, not only claimed that it would 'do' in ten years what others had taken a hundred years to achieve, but also endlessly boasted of its "nationalist" credentials. Hence, it not only never shied away from whipping up nationalist sentiments and frenzy, but also went to great lengths to vilify the democratic forces of the country as "anti-national elements" and "foreign agents and stooges."

If democracy in the Nepalese society has had to overcome attacks from the right, it also has had to face challenges from the left, i.e. the communists. Communists, including Nepalese communists, have traditionally derided multiparty democracy as "bourgeois democracy," "capitalist democracy" or even "old democracy," contrasting it with the "New Democracy" of the communists. The one-party communist state, in the name of New Democracy or New People's Democracy, People's Republic or dictatorship of the proletariat, has been the ideal for the communists. Thus, the Nepalese society, a semi-feudal and semi-colonial one according to the communists, sometime in the future—the time depends on the fancy of the individual or the party concerned—is to ultimately make the transition to socialism and communism. Their ideological positioning has meant that Nepalese communists have often had to take recourse to elaborate sophistry to justify their participation in democratic politics. The Unified Communist Party of Nepal (Maoist), after entering into peace accord and democratic politics following a decade-long "people's war", has come to justify its current democratic "interlude" as the phase for the completion of the "capitalist revolution," prior to ultimately embarking upon socialism and communism. (Of course, debates within the Maoists show that there are some in the party who would like to considerably shorten this period of "capitalist revolution" and embark, with almost immediate effect, upon the phase of the "People's Republic," i.e. the one-party rule of the communists. The important issue in this context is what the Maoists, or any other communist party for that matter, would do if they had the power to impose their rule over the entire society. Would they still pay "lip service" to democracy, or would they impose their one-party dictatorship? That would be the ultimate "democratic test" for all communists and communist parties.)

The post-1990 second democratic phase has seen the prominent involvement of communist parties in Nepalese politics. They have been in the parliament in significant numbers, even occasionally forming the government by themselves or in coalition with other political parties. Among these communist parties, one of the smaller parties even contested parliamentary elections under the name Communist Party of Nepal (Democratic). Another party, one of the largest and most powerful of the communist parties in the country, namely the Communist Party of Nepal (Unified Marxist-Leninist) adopted in 1992 "People's Multiparty Democracy" as its party line. A prominent and powerful leader of the party recently came forth with the extraordinary statement that "we are communists, hence we believe in democratic norms and values" (Nepal 2008: 7).

The significant role the communist parties have come to play in Nepalese politics can be seen from the composition of the Constituent Assembly elected in 2008. The 601-member Constituent Assembly elected for drafting the constitution has around 60 percent of its members from various communist parties. This includes the Unified Communist Party of Nepal (Maoist) with more than one-third members, the Communist Party of Nepal (Unified Marxist-Leninist) with over one-sixth members, as well as members from several other smaller communist parties. This has led to apprehension—and this especially with regard to the rebel-turned-legitimate political party of the Maoists—about whether the Constituent Assembly will be able to draft a constitution that protects individual rights and freedoms. Or, will democratic norms and values come to be restricted in the name of some overriding "group" or "collective" interest. This apprehension, of course, stems from the traditional communist intolerance for differing and opposing views, one indication of which is the Maoists' attitude towards the media.

The fourth estate, i.e. the media has been quite rightly dubbed as one of the success stories of the post-1990 democratic order, with the sprouting in the private sector of broadsheet dailies, including in the English language, FM radio stations and television channels. The often raucous and rambunctious post-1990 Nepalese media could be compared with the free media of any other democratic society. On the other hand, the Maoists, in order to impose their authority over the general populace, have often had to employ brutal and savage means, even going to the extent of killing those who opposed them. Those facing the wrath of the Maoists have included the media and mediapersons. The state of affairs created by the Maoists has been such that journalists have been reported to have practiced self-censorship, so as to avoid persecution by the Maoists. The actions of the Maoists can be compared with that of the then King Gyanendra following his royal coup of February 1, 2005. After the coup, Gyanendra's regime not only blocked telephone lines, including mobile services, but also imposed severe restrictions on the media. Army personnel were stationed at media houses, with the aim of censuring dissenting voices. The curbs put on the media of course proved counterproductive in the long run, leading ultimately to not only the toppling of Gyanendra's regime but also to an end to the over two-centuries old institution of monarchy itself.

In this context, the one-party system espoused by Communists has not only meant curbs on political parties but also on the media. Communist countries like China are well known not only for their restrictions on press and publication but also for their restrictions on one of most popular innovations of recent times, namely the Internet. Nepalese communists like the Maoists have also persecuted and even killed mediapersons, this even after entering into peace accord with the government. Maoist activities have led to the closure for some days of the publication of private sector broadsheet dailies, something that had not happened even during Gyanendra's autocratic royal regime.

The Liberal Individual

The attacks upon secular modernity in recent times have meant that the individual espoused by liberal modernity has come to be seen as not universal but as a historical construct, a particular product of our times, even a "philosophical fiction." The issues related to ethnicity, language, culture and religion that have in recent times come to the forefront have led to "revivalist" movements around the world. An observer has pointed to the nativist or sons of the soil movements in neighbouring India, as well as to the rise of nativist, linguistic and regional politics therein (Gupta 1995). Democratic India over the last half century has not only given way to a more decentralised structure, with power being devolved away from the centre, but also no longer does one political party have monopoly at the centre as in the past. Gone are the days of absolute majority for any one party at the centre, and coalitions of almost two dozen political parties at the centre have become the norm nowadays. The modernist aspirations of early and mid-twentieth century India have given way to more revivalist practices. Today, fewer politicians share the elite cosmopolitan English-speaking urban, and urbane, liberal background exemplified by India's first Prime Minister Jawaharlal Nehru. Instead, a growing number of parliamentarians are earthy in manner, populist and anti-intellectual by inclination, as well as unsophisticated in their political utterances (Chiriyankandath 1997: 20).

Given that the liberal individual is a historical construct and is not universal, the views regarding liberty and freedom can vary across cultures and societies. In this context, there has been pointed the differing views on liberty between the modern and the ancient world. The ancient Greeks, for instance, were not only aware of the "national" character of their thinking, in contrast to the universal, but their idea of liberty and freedom was also in sharp contrast to the modern one. Whereas for modern men, liberty signifies a protected sphere of non-interference or independence under the rule of law, for the ancients it meant entitlement to a voice in collective decision-making. The dominant idea of freedom among the ancient Greeks was not the idea of an assured space of individual independence. For the Greeks, as perhaps for the Romans, the idea of freedom was applied as naturally to communities—where it meant self-rule, or the absence of external control—as it was to individuals. Even in its application to individuals, it rarely connoted any immunity from control by the community, but only an entitlement to participation in its deliberations (Gray 1998: 3).

If we accept that liberty implies a say within the group to which one belongs, and not non-interference regarding the way one conducts one's affairs individually, this gives rise to a wholly new perspective, a way of looking at things. This goes beyond mere appearances and utterances, the way one dresses, one speaks or one chews one's food or sips one's tea. Leaders of a particular group can, in this context, claim for the group as a whole external protections from the outside world, while at the same time going on to impose, in the name of the interest of the group as a whole, internal restrictions on the individual members of the group concerned. They can buttress their argument by stating, quite correctly, that the individual rights and freedoms espoused by liberal societies are not absolute in themselves. After all, no society tolerates absolute freedom even of conscience and of speech, and no society reduces that sphere to zero. The question here clearly becomes a matter of degree (Schumpeter 1954: 271).

The argument that the individual should forsake his or her rights in the name of the group or community, for the sake of a larger "good" is hardly novel of course. We do it all the time, for the family, for a group of friends, for a larger collective like the nation, etc. In this context, we may even forsake our "present" for the sake of an imagined for better, albeit unknown, future. Communists, for instance, justify their so-called revolutionary violence in the name of an abstract ideal of the future. They have, in the name of this ideal, even gone to the extent of killing of what they have called class enemies. The "revolutionary violence" unleashed by communists against their "class enemies" during the course of the last century could even be termed "classicide," similar to genocide or ethnocide. Also, after attaining power, communist rulers around the world have gone on to impose draconian measures severely restricting the rights and freedoms of the ruled in the name of a larger collective "class." The populace, in the communist scheme of things, are supposed to forego many of their rights for the greater "good," even though this good may be in some imagined for distant future.

The National Context

Of course, in today's age of nationalism the group *par excellence* is the nation-state itself, "the paragon of human association and aspiration" (Anaya 1996: 14). This state of affairs is said to have originated with the Treaty of Westphalia of 1648, with the division of the world into clearly delineated jurisdictions, i.e. nation-states regarded as the organising principle of politics (Camilleri and Falk 1992: 141). Nation-states over the years have come to claim from their citizens exclusivity over all other allegiances and loyalties, superseding all other "groups" like the family, village, clan, tribe, caste or religion. Nation-states have gone to war against each other, and sometimes even against their own citizens. They have killed, maimed and displaced countless number of peoples, all in the name of the supreme "national interest."

In this context, even when they do not explicitly say so, authors who regard sociology as the study of "societies" have in mind the societies associated with modernity. In conceptualising them, they think of quite clearly delimited systems, which have their inner unity. Understood in this way, "societies" are plainly nation-states (Giddens 1990: 13). Therefore, it does not become surprising to talk, with their clearly delineated boundaries as well as characteristics, of "societies" like the "Nepalese society," "Indian society," "Chinese society," "American society," etc. Our own "Nepalese society" has given rise also to "Nepalese origin," with all its racist and xenophobic connotations, as well as to "Nepalese originality" and "uniquely Nepalese." The erstwhile Panchayat system, for instance, claimed of itself as being representative of Nepalese originality, as well as of being unique to the Nepal Himalaya. Today, with a new constitution being drafted and Nepal being transformed from a unitary to a federal state, we can often hear political leaders of all stripes talking of not only a constitution but also a federal structure with "Nepalese originality" or "Nepalese characteristic."

The nation-state today has not only claimed monopoly over the legitimate use of force, but there is also the extensive concentration of political, military and ideological power in modern nation-states. The nation-state is also a "moral community," in that it is not only demanding of fealty and loyalty from its citizens, often to the exclusion of others, but it also prescribes for its citizens standards of behaviour and actions to follow. Besides, it also demarcates those who belong, the "us" from those who do not, i.e. "them." Citizenship, therefore, is an inherently group-differentiated notion. To distribute rights and benefits on the basis of citizenship is to treat people differentially on the basis of their group membership. With citizenship comes a sense of solidarity and belonging, even an identity, given that citizenship is not just a legal status, defined by a set of rights and responsibilities, but also an identity, an expression of one's membership in a political community (Kymlicka 1995: 124-125, 192). Thus, it has been said that the range, i.e. the number of people within which the moral code is applied has narrowed since the Middle Ages, precisely because of the result of the rise of nationalism (Durant 1954: 55). Nation-states have often claimed inviolability from even human rights principles and instruments.

Nation-states have gone to great lengths to create, as well as to protect, their "national identity," and also the sense of national consciousness, solidarity and community. Even those who espouse liberal values have traditionally conceived of the political system associated with such liberalism within the boundaries of the nation-state. The appeal of nationalism is such that groups other than those conventionally regarded in political science as nation-states or "nations," too, have come to conceive of themselves as nations. When a well known Nepalese indigenous nationality intellectual describes the Nepalese indigenous nationality groups as being a "nationalist" force, he is ascribing what could be called an uniquely modern phenomenon to groups that are even today traditional, even pre-modern, in their social structure (Gurung 2001: 224). Thus, it is not surprising in the Nepalese context to hear of indigenous nations (i.e. the individual indigenous nationality groups as nations, for instance the Newar Nation, Khambuwan Nation, Magarat Nation, Limbuwan Nation, etc.), nationalities, i.e. groups on the verge of or with the potential of becoming nations, *Madhesi* Nation, Hindu Nation, etc. Beyond one can see the Nation of Islam, Christian Nation, Black Nationalism, Lesbian Nation, among others. In this context, there are a whole range of groups that in today's age of nationalism have come to claim of themselves—not unjustifiably—as "nations." I say not unjustifiably primarily for two reasons, in keeping with the argument of political scientist Walker Connor.

One, most—if not all—of the so-called nation-states in the world are not nation-states but "nations-within-a-state" or multinational states. If the two entities the nation and the state essentially coincided, it would not be inappropriate to use the term nation-state. But given that most of the existing states in the world comprise of multiple groups or nations, it is more correct to refer to them as multinational states. This of course gives rise to a host of issues, including ones to do with semantics, or the proper use of words. The 'United Nations' is obviously a misnomer, it should be correctly called the 'United States.' The discipline International Relations should be designated Inter-State Relations. Even the International Court of Justice should be correctly called the Inter-State Court of Justice and the International Monetary Fund the Inter-State Monetary Fund (Connor 1994: 96-97)!

Two, by referring to groups other than states as "tribes," "ethnic groups," etc., while reserving "nationalism" to describe attachment to states, we underestimate the emotional bond that the former exert upon individuals. There is also the view that "tribes," in addition to being "lowly," connote a primitive, evolutionary stage in human organisation. In keeping with the modern idea of linear progress, tribes are viewed as something of the past. They are decidedly not seen as the wave of the future. This leads to the presumption that the loyalty of the individual will assuredly over time be transferred from the part, which is actually the nation but called the tribe, to the whole, actually the state but called the nation (Ibid.: 108).

As regards the Nepalese context, the Nepalese state, especially during the Panchayat years, had gone to great lengths to subsume all other identities under a homogenising Nepalese "national" identity. Even today there is the tendency to see the multinational aspirations of groups like the indigenous nationalities as communal, disintegrative, separatist, etc. Groups like the indigenous nationalities are seen as not befitting the rights—for instance, the right to self-determination, the extensive rights to manage and control their own affairs—that Nepal as a full-blooded nation-state has. They are regarded as "lowly," "sub-national," "parochial," not on the same equal footing as Nepal as a nation-state. The situation is compounded by the use of the two words in the Khas-Nepali language, namely *jati* and *rastra*. Although both these words can be—and often have been—translated into English as nation, there is the tendency to use *jati* in the sense of 'ethnic group,' 'tribe' or 'people,' while *rastra* refers to the nation. Thus, groups like the indigenous nationalities are regarded as merely *jatis* and not *rastras*.

Building Nations

Like Nepal, states around the world have traditionally been constructed around a cultural core, thus disregarding the multicultural/multinational nature of the territories they have inhabited. This cultural core is what makes the 'nation' in the nation-state. The argument, in this context, that the so-called non-cultural conception of national membership is often said to be what distinguishes the 'civic' or 'constitutional' nationalism of countries like the United States from illiberal 'ethnic' nationalism is erroneous. The immigrants to the United States must not only pledge allegiance to democratic principles, but they must also learn the language and history of their new society. Many have been lured over the years to the United States by the American Dream, but these migrants have to make sure that they dream their American Dream in English! What distinguishes 'civic' nations from 'ethnic' nations is not the absence of any cultural component to national identity, but rather the fact that anyone can integrate into the common culture, regardless of race or colour (Kymlicka 1995: 24).

If we accept the right of varied groups to claim of themselves as nations—and there is no reason why we should not—it gives rise to several issues. The first is obviously the challenge posed to the around two hundred entities in the world that have won general acceptance as nation-states. The second is that it is one thing to conceive of nations and another to make them. The process of making them or "constructing" them has its own dynamic. One is the practice of stressing of heterogeneity or difference vis-à-vis other groups, while emphasising on homogeneity within one's own group. Perhaps the starkest manifestation of this is the standardisation of language, where the several "dialects" are systematically eliminated to create one standard language of the group. As mentioned in the previous chapter, in Nepal groups like the indigenous nationalities have already embarked upon this process.

Another is the creating of boundaries, thus demarcating with clarity and precision the territory that belongs to one, and to which one belongs. This takes the form of well-defined borders, not to mention the armed personnel to man those borders against outsiders. Referring to the indigenous peoples of the Americas and elsewhere, S. James Anaya has mentioned that the various indigenous groups therein did not traditionally conceive of themselves in this exclusivist sense. Rather they, at least prior to European contact, typically have been organised primarily by tribal or kinship ties, have had decentralised political structures often linked in confederations and have enjoyed shared or overlapping spheres of territorial control. The Native American indigenous peoples as the Iroquois Confederacy and the Creek Indians do not represent singular political or national identities for the people they encompass. Both traditionally had—and to a great extent continue to have—segmentary political structures defined by kinship, geography and function (Anaya 1996: 15, 79).

The political philosophy for the Iroquois Confederacy is expressed in the Great Law of Peace, which describes a great tree with roots extending in the four cardinal directions to all peoples of the earth. All are invited to follow the roots to the tree and join in peaceful coexistence and cooperation under its great long leaves. The Great Law of Peace promotes unity among individuals, families, clans and nations while at the same time upholding the integrity of diverse identities and spheres of autonomy. Similar ideals have been expressed by leaders of other indigenous groups in contemporary appeals to international bodies. These conceptions outside the mold of classical Western liberalism would appear to provide a more appropriate foundation for understanding humanity, its aspirations and its political development than the model of a world divided into exclusive, monolithic communities (Ibid.: 79).

As regards the Nepalese context, the issue when the Gorkhali-Nepalese elites began to conceive of their state in spatially coherent terms is debatable. The Gorkhali records of the eighteenth and early nineteenth century often couch references to the Gorkhali-Nepalese state, as well as other states, in terms of such metaphors as *dhungo*, literally stone. Such references clearly pertain to a notion of the state that was distinct from the King, or the rulers. Although some scholars have suggested that in referring to the state as such the Gorkhali-Nepalese elites of the time were emphasising the territorial integrity of the state in the modern sense of the term, the evidence from various parts of the country does not bear this out (Michael 1999: 287). A historian, in this context, has pointed to the Prime Minister Bhimsen Thapa's belated understanding of the very European, as well as the very modern, concept of border, and his perception of the roots of British concern about the Nepal-India border, that enabled him to negotiate with the British for the return to Nepal of parts of the tarai following the Anglo-Nepal war of 1814-16 (Stiller 1989: 106). Today, of course, the sanctity and inviolability of national borders is an essential element of political discourse, and few dare question it. Nepalese nationalists continue to raise hue and cry against the alleged encroachment of the country's border by its neighbours, especially its southern neighbour India. Groups like the indigenous nationalities have come forth with their own "borders" that precisely delineate their federal states/ autonomous regions within the territory of Nepal.

Nations are often seen as a large extended family, originating from a common ancestor. The state can be seen as a mother ("Mother Nepal") and one's fellow citizens as one's brethren, i.e. brothers and sisters. The themes of ethnic purity or racial purity are not uncommon to nationalist discourse. By invoking history nations can not only make claims over the present but also over the past. Nations are seen as existing throughout time, from the hoary past to the indefinite future. Thus, Nepalese nationalists can trace Nepal's roots to remote antiquity, claiming that Nepal has existed over centuries, even millennia (see Serchan 2007: 20-21). The 'totalising' discourse of nationalism makes claims over time, i.e. history and also space, i.e. geography. Indeed, history is often invoked so as to establish and legitimise control over space or geography. This, in a way, is the phenomenon of the creation of the nation-state.*

---

* In this context, even the way a state chooses to name itself can confer upon it a legitimacy and primacy that is belittling of others. A historian has pointed to the naming of 'India' following independence from British colonial rule in 1947. After Jawaharlal Nehru and the Indian National Congress Party adopted as their country's name 'India,' Pakistan's founding father Mohammed Ali Jinnah "was absolutely furious" that they, i.e. Nehru and the Congress Party were going to call themselves India. The use of the word implied a subcontinental primacy that Pakistan would never accept. It also flew in the face of history, since 'India' originally referred exclusively to the territory in the vicinity of the Indus river, with which the word is cognate. Hence, it was largely outside India but largely within Pakistan. Jinnah had apparently been under the impression that neither of the two states that arose following the end of British rule would want to adopt the British title of 'India' (Keay 2000: 56-57).

Nevertheless, if real-world populations, in the face of a homogenising universalism, continue to find sustenance and strength from their respective groups and communities, groups and communities they can "get their arms around," the issue regarding its compatibility with democratic norms and practices becomes not insignificant and unimportant. After all, democracy in our times is essentially national in character. One can, in this context, question whether the Western liberal individual is merely "a philosophical fiction of abstract individuality," to be submerged, if not annihilated in the interests of the group as a whole. The question is pertinent given that nation-states have not shied away from imposing restrictions on the individual rights of their citizens in the name of an overriding national interest. More importantly, citizens themselves have been willing to sacrifice their individual rights and freedoms in the name of peace, national security, etc. This has happened especially during times of distress and difficulties. A liberal democracy like Britain during World War I went to the extent of executing its soldiers deserting the war effort as "traitors." In the 1950s, faced with the spectre of communism, the United States carried out a McCarthian witch-hunt against its own citizens accusing them of "Un-American" activities.

After the 9/11 attacks of 2001, developed democracies like the United States went on to put curbs on civil liberties and freedoms in the name of the so-called war on terror. This took the form of laws like the Patriot Act and even the sanctioning of torture and the setting up of the Guantanamo Bay prison with the aim of incarcerating "terror suspects" without fair trial and recourse to the courts for the rest of their natural lives. The American people have been willing, for their own safety and in the name of national security, to turn a blind eye to, if not condone, all these acts and activities.

In Nepal, after the then King Gyanendra on February 1, 2005 usurped power from the political parties, the general populace was more than willing to give him the benefit of doubt, in the hope that the King would restore peace and security to an insurgency-ravaged country. This happened even with Gyanendra curtailing civil and political rights and arresting and imprisoning political leaders and civil society figures. For the ordinary men and women apparently all these were sacrifices worth making if the King could deliver them from the insecurity, deaths and destruction related to the decade-long Maoist insurgency.

The Unified Communist Party of Nepal (Maoist) might have had few qualms about the violence it had unleashed during its "people's war." For the Maoists, no doubt the end justified the means, and even the most despicable acts could be glossed over as "revolutionary violence" and necessary in the implacable march of history. But even the supposedly democratic political parties and their leaders showed scant consideration regarding the means to be employed in their fight against Maoist "terrorists." The democratically elected government imposed emergency to fight the Maoists, thus ensuring that the state apparatus, especially the army, would not have to be accountable for human rights abuses. Given that Nepal is still not a fully "written" society, the horrors committed by the Nepalese state, especially the army, in its own "war on terror" have not been fully documented, and possibly never will be. But there is no denying the state terror and the gross human rights violations, and anyone killed by the state could be called a Maoist.

The summary executions, arbitrary detention and imprisonment without trial, not to mention the countless humiliations that had to be endured by the general populace, were a feature of the Nepalese state's "war on terror." The "democratic" political leadership who had spent years in opposition against the Panchayat, enduring unlawful imprisonment, torture and all kinds of abuse and harassment, showed few qualms regarding the means when they themselves became the government. Their espousal of the principles of liberal democracy remained just that, principle and not practice. All this no doubt had to do with the survival of the larger "group"—group here referring to the system, i.e. the political system—with which their own individual fortunes were interlinked and dependant.*

The around 200 so-called nation-states in the world have given scant consideration to the means as far as their own national interests have been concerned. Jingoistic nationalism of the 'my country right or wrong' variety has often been the norm, and political leaders have been more than willing to whip up "national" sentiments, even frenzy, among the populace. The mentality of the herd or mob has never been far from modern nation-states. Given this, it is not surprising if Nepalese politicians find "national" slogans among the most attractive to "lure" the people and sway public opinion. National "pride" can find expression not only in the political realm, but also through activities like sports and music. "Sports nationalism" can find manifestation in sports like football and cricket and in events like the South Asian Games held in Kathmandu in 1999, during which the "national" feelings of sports-loving Nepalese youths was in full display. (The misbehaviour of local Nepalese fans towards the opposition, etc. during sports events like international football matches has even raised the possibility of Nepal being penalised and being deprived of the opportunity of hosting any international tournaments [*The Himalayan Times* 2009: 12].) And although the youth in Nepal may be fully under the sway of Western musical styles like rock, pop, rap, etc., these youths have nevertheless been eager to pay

---

* The savagery of the Maoist rebels was matched by the violence and lack of accountability shown by the Nepalese state apparatus like the army and police. The army and police both adopted a take-no-prisoners policy, and were dismissive of the principles of war that demand the humane treatment of combatants. Red Cross instructors who had conducted courses with Nepalese Army soldiers stated that they found it a challenge to explain why the army could not behave like the Maoists (Dixit 2003: 306). The soldiers were apparently forgetting that the state has instruments like laws and physical facilities like police posts and prisons through which it can take "legitimate" action against all kinds of opposition, including those engaged in violence.

their homage to 'Mother Nepal.' One can find in the lyrics of young Nepalese singers-songwriters words and phrases like 'Nepal,' 'Nepali,' 'My heart is Nepali,' etc.

A Nepalese Democracy?

The emphasis on 'uniquely Nepali' and all its associated revivalist practices stand, if not in contradistinction, at least in ambivalence towards the West, towards the modern. The political system of the Panchayat was after all born out of these very nativist impulses, with the ideologues of the system claiming the Panchayat as suited to the air, water and the soil of the country. Following the democratic change of 1990, a Hindu conservative writer came forth with the suggestion that the King and the people should gather at *Tundikhel*, an open public ground, and conduct the affairs of the state (Naraharinath 2000: 3). This—a form of direct democracy?—was apparently offered as a 'Hindu' alternative to the western representative democratic system. In this context, it may be worth remembering the comment of a member of the Indian Constituent Assembly elected following independence from British colonial rule. The "mortified" member, referring to the Indian constitution made by the Constituent Assembly, stated that they had wanted the music of traditional Indian instruments like the *veena* and *sitar*, but had instead been treated to the music of an English band (quoted in Khilnani 1994: 200)!

Nevertheless, it is not only India, despite some of its citizens' aversion to "English band," that has adopted the modern political system of multiparty democracy. India, after all, prides itself in being "the largest democracy in the world." Even a country like Iran following the 1979 Islamic Revolution, "the first postmodern revolution," is said to have little new to offer in the way of its political system. Except for the "Guardian Council" of religious leaders to "guide" the polity, the Iranian system is said to contain features that are similar to any developed democracy of the West. Representative democracy with competitive multiparty elections has become the norm throughout the world. "Direct democracy" may be feasible in small groups, for instance indigenous nationality groups like the Kusunda and Raute numbering in the hundreds. The important condition in this regard is, of course, that all members of the concerned group, including the women, should have equal opportunity to participate in the direct democracy. Also, instead of elections, the leaders of the group can be chosen through consensus, with the important caveat that such consent should be real and not manufactured. The election of a candidate unopposed from the remote mountainous district of Manang in the parliamentary elections of 1991 can be illustrative in this regard. This is despite the fact that Manang, a district inhabited predominantly by the indigenous nationality group Manange-Gurung, has a population of less than 10,000.

A feature of representative democracies is political parties, and developing democracies like Nepal are no exception to this. One can quibble at the vices of political parties, and Nepalese political parties have not been immune from the partisanship, gamesmanship and one-upmanship that seem to afflict political parties everywhere. After monsoon rains created havoc in the eastern tarai in 2008, the President, Vice-President and the Prime Minister, all from different political parties, went, at considerable government expense, on separate trips of the flood-ravaged areas. (There were also government ministers from various political parties going on visits to the affected areas.) This may have been due to heartfelt sympathies for the victims, but was more to do with the scoring of political points over their rivals, or to be seen as not 'lacking' in the "game" of politics. This kind of gamesmanship will no doubt continue, and it will be extremely difficult for any political party to praise, or refrain from criticising, its rivals, no matter how good the latter's policies, programmes and performance are. In this context, political parties, despite all their shortcomings, appear today as "a necessary evil." That they need not be a feature of only democratic societies can also be seen from our own experience. After the third amendment to the "partyless" Panchayat constitution following the referendum of 1980 allowed for direct elections through adult franchise to the legislature, i.e. the *Rastriya Panchayat*, there appeared groups or factions within the *Rastriya Panchayat.* The groups were not only engaged in activities like the ouster of the Prime Minister through voting, but there also appeared real ideological differences between the concerned groups. The groups, one could say, were embryonic parties in the making and, given time, could well have evolved into ideologically based political parties around the "liberals" and the "hardliners" in the polity.

If we accept that an appropriate political system in our times has to have the "minimal" requirements of competition and participation, political parties and the like, should we take the next step and also accept that such a political system or democracy should be "liberal," that is it should hold certain rights of the individual as sacrosanct and thus inalienable? That we accept there are certain individual rights, rights that have also been called negative freedoms, such as not to be persecuted for one's views and beliefs, not to be physically abused and tortured, not to have to undergo unlawful detention and imprisonment, that are applicable to all societies and cultures? If we accept this, then these liberal rights become inviolable and not to be infringed upon. They cannot be taken away, in the name of the group, national interest, national security, etc.

The emphasis on individuality, on individual viewpoints, even on individual fancies and quirkiness means accepting the diversity within a particular group. After all, as Bhikhu Parekh has correctly pointed out, every culture is also internally plural and reflects a continuing conversation between its different traditions and strands of thought (Parekh 1999). Therefore, despite what the self-appointed guardians of a culture might say, tolerance for differing and dissenting viewpoints within a particular culture or group becomes the norm. Liberals can argue that there is a virtue in doing so. As it is not only individuals but also groups that have to adapt to inevitably changing situations and circumstances, the differing voices within a group can provide the choice towards this adaptation. Thus, ideas that may be regarded as novel and out of the way, even bizarre, within a particular group at a particular time may, in another situation and circumstance, prove to be useful for the survival and the continuity of the group as a whole.

Of course, the liberal argument can be countered by saying that, given the changing situations and circumstances, cultures and ways of life regarded as not useful at one time may prove their usefulness at another time. Hence, "culturists" might argue for the need for the preserving of cultures, even of "freezing" them so that they might be useful at some time in the future. And these cultures can well be illiberal ones, that is they may give emphasis on the interest of the group than on the rights of the individual. An instance of culture being discarded and being taken up again as "good" at another time is of course the current "revivalist" practices among the indigenous nationality groups of Nepal. Under the influence of a centralising Hindu Nepalese state, Nepalese indigenous nationalities in the past had adopted practices in consonance with the ruling Hindu "high" castes of the Nepalese society. This was in accordance with the overall trend in South Asia, a trend that has been called as Sanskritisation (Srinivas 1966). Today, of course, few would condone the Hindu caste system or the harshly patriarchal structures in Hindu societies. This has meant that indigenous nationalities who in the past had discarded their own customs and practices as lowly are today reverting back to their "original" practices.

In this context, any attempt to discard a culture and way of life as useless can be regarded as foolhardy. Even the liberal "project" remains only one among the many to provide the basis for a good society. Given this, it may simply be naive to forsake all our inherited cultural capital and stake everything on the liberal enterprise. Nevertheless, tolerating not only inter- but also intra-group diversity means simply accepting reality, the reality of a plural world. There can always be the temptation to brook no difference in the name of the supposed welfare of the larger group. The assertion that only one has access to the truth leads to intolerance, if not worse. Although a group-nation has every right to protect its language, culture and way of life, this need not, and does not have to be, at the cost of the rights of the individual members. Nepalese indigenous nationality groups can afford to be tolerant of the differing voices within their particular group. Indeed, given the "we-feeling" among the indigenous nationality groups, individual members have been voluntarily willing to forsake their individual interests for the larger welfare of the group. For indigenous nationality individuals, their ascriptive collective identities remain of pivotal importance, around which their own lives revolve.

As individuals seek nourishment and sustenance from their own cultures, indeed live worthwhile lives by virtue of being part of their own cultures, they also through their activities enrich the cultures of which they are a part. Groups and their leaders can do worse than attempting to stifle the creativity of their individual members. Even though states have always imposed restrictions on their individual citizens, there do appear some red lines not to be crossed in this regard. A country like Turkey has made "insulting" what it calls Turkishness a punishable criminal offence. This has restricted the political space for the expression of views and opinions. It has also encouraged zealots, i.e. the self-proclaimed guardians of a culture to give vent to highly intolerant positions. The balancing of group-based national identities with individual rights remains a delicate task. It is one of the challenges of our times with nationalism and democracy both as powerful discourses to guide and motivate countless millions of peoples around the world.

6

Modernity and Marginalisation: The World at the Periphery

Modernity put human reason on a pedestal, hoping that it would ameliorate all the ills of the world. When the claims of human reason replaced those of tradition, they appeared to offer a certitude greater than that provided by preexisting dogma (Giddens 1990: 39). There was no doubt the hope that reason would relieve human beings from not only ignorance but also from all uncertainties. But the wholesale reflexivity of modernity, a reflexivity that also includes reflection upon the nature of reflection itself, actually subverts reason, at any rate where reason is understood as the gaining of certain knowledge. Modernity is constituted in and through reflexively applied knowledge, but at the same time we can never be sure that any given element of that knowledge will not be revised. This is a deeply unsettling outlook. Even philosophers who have most staunchly defended the claims of science to certitude, such as Karl Popper, acknowledge that all science rests upon shifting sand. In science nothing is certain, and nothing can be proved, even if scientific endeavour provides us with the most dependable information about the world to which we can aspire. In the heart of the world of hard science, modernity floats free. This is the end or dissolution of foundationalism and foundational knowledge. We have come to discover that nothing can be known with any certainty, since all pre-existing "foundations" of epistemology have been shown to be unreliable. Also, history is devoid of *telos*, of teleology and consequently no version of progress can plausibly be defended. Modernity replaced divine providence by providential progress, but today there is loss of belief in the very idea of progress (Ibid.: 38-48).

As relativism of knowledge is built into modern thought, claims to certitude cannot be made without relapsing into dogma. The more we know the more we become aware of the limitation as well as the fallibility of human knowledge; questioning and scepticism are the very essence of reason. The positivistic pretensions of nineteenth century social sciences have proven to be just that pretensions. In this context, it is noteworthy that Marxism has been called a religion and Marx a prophet (Schumpeter 1954: 5). Marxism itself, of course, added a class dimension to what was regarded as universal human reason. Thus, in place of a supposedly single, indivisible and universal reality, there was the reality of the bourgeoisie and the proletariat, the capitalist and the working class and the exploiter and the exploited. Today's politics of recognition also emphasises upon the fragmentary nature of reality, with the myriad perspectives of diverse peoples and cultures, regions and religions around the world. Hence, in place of a modernity that stresses upon uniformity and homogeneity, the world today is seen as being postmodern.

Globalisation's "Flat" World

Globalisation would have us believe that its fruits, if not today then sometime in the future, will be distributed equitably among all the countries, regions and peoples of the world. The entire world will have the material conditions of life at present being enjoyed by the developed countries of the West. This hope seems to have blinded some to the fact that just as universalisation means uniformity, globalisation implies homogenisation and the destroying of diversity, i.e. the varied languages, cultures and ways of life of the world. It implies that all the peoples of the world should speak one language and follow the same culture and way of life, thus becoming "one." It puts one cultural enterprise above and at the exclusion of all others, thus tying all of humanity's future to it. This what could be called a purely economic outlook to things has led to comments like it is the deprivation at the periphery or unequal development that generates, particularly in the exploited and backward regions, the consciousness of a regional identity and sense of autonomy or independence, which often takes a "nationalistic" form (Bhattarai 2003: 150). The above comment by a well known ideologue and political leader of the Unified Communist Party of Nepal (Maoist) implies that if there was equitable economic development throughout the world, a lack that the Maoist ideologue-cum-leader not unsurprisingly attributes to capitalism, there would be no cultural or "nationalist" upheavals that we are witnessing at present. In the Marxist scheme of things, the current concerns over culture and multiculturalism are merely minor irritants in the forward march towards socialism and communism.

Communists like the Maoists, while railing against the West as imperialists, and against the present globalisation as neo-colonisation, can nevertheless be ambivalent vis-à-vis the current developing state of affairs. A passage from one of their official documents, where they talk about the profit motive that is driving the present globalisation as well as the special circumstances created by it, can be illuminating in this regard.

> First, in the name of acquiring profit by relating high technology with the cheap labour of the large masses, it (i.e. globalisation) has created awareness among the populace to go from the world of necessity to the world of freedom. Second, the improvements in information technology, especially in the electronic sector, have made the world a global village, with the consequence that developments, positive or negative, in one part of the world have impact in other parts of the world. This has increased to a surprising and extraordinary extent. Third, in the name of acquiring profit, imperialism has led to the production and distribution of arms and weapons on a global scale, which has indirectly laid the ground for the preparation of the world people's war on a global scale. Fourth, the uncontrolled production and the globalisation of the social process of production are preparing with an extraordinary

> swiftness the material infrastructure for the communist principle of work according to ability and distribution according to necessity. Fifth, and most importantly, by attenuating to its maximum class contradictions, especially the contradiction between imperialism and oppressed nations and peoples, imperialism is preparing with increased and accelerated pace the objective conditions for revolution among the 80 percent of the people of the world (CPN [Maoist] 2006: 165).*

The above passage, which I have translated from the original Khas-Nepali, seems to imply that globalisation is the obverse of communism, and the present stage of capitalist globalisation will ultimately lead to the global communism of the future. Like capitalism, communism, too,

---

* Compare this with what Marx and Engels wrote in the *Communist Manifesto*: "The bourgeoisie has played an extremely revolutionary role upon the stage of history....The bourgeoisie was the first to show us what human activity is capable of achieving. It has executed works more marvelous than the building of Egyptian pyramids, Roman aqueducts, and Gothic cathedrals....the bourgeoisie drags all the nations, even the most barbarian, into the orbit of civilization....It has brought huge cities into being....Moreover, just as it has made the country dependent on the town, so it has made the barbarian and the semi-barbarian nations dependent upon the civilized nations, the peasant peoples upon the industrialized peoples, the East upon the West....During its reign of scarce a century, the bourgeoisie has created more powerful, more stupendous forces of production than all preceding generations rolled into one. The subjugation of the forces of nature, the invention of machinery, the application of chemistry to industry and agriculture, steamships, railways, electric telegraphs, the clearing of whole continents for cultivation, the making of navigable waterways, huge populations springing up as if by magic out of the earth—what earlier generations had the remotest inkling that such productive powers slumbered within the womb of associated labor?" (see Mills 1962: 48-51). The eulogising, almost rhapsodic, tone of the above paragraph is not surprising, given that Marx and Engels praised the historic and progressive role played by capitalism. It is of course not a coincidence that Marx and Engels's most famous work has as its title *Capital*.

envisages the optimum exploitation of nature for the material benefit of humankind. It also, in the name of universality, aims to impose its own homogeneity throughout the world. In this regard, both capitalism and communism remain as the twin products of modernity. They both look towards a future of material abundance (well-fed and well-dressed men and women, squeaky clean concrete-and-glass skyscrapers, trains running with clockwork precision, for instance), for which uniformity and homogeneity will be small prices to pay.

But this vision of an utopia of material affluence has several problems. It is based on the belief that there are no limits to growth. This belief in limitless growth, however, raises two issues that are inter-related to each other. The first is that the planet earth can sustain unlimited growth forever. This, in effect, means that the material conditions of life at present within the reach of only the people of the Western developed countries will be accessible to the over six billion people of the world. This means the creation of many "Americas" around the world, with the American way of life available to all peoples. The second issue related to this is that there will always be technological breakthroughs to sustain such growth. That is even if the earth's resources cannot do so, human technological ingenuity will overcome such constraints and sustain material growth forever in the future. Thus, humans will invent new fuels to replace the rapidly depleting fossil fuels, they may even discover new earth-like planets to inhabit and settle on, and so on and on.

The advocates of a "flat" world can point to market globalisation's penetration into even the farthest corners of the world, and how it is "positively" impacting upon the lives of peoples therein. Indeed, globalisation's "dazzle" can even be felt in a poor country like Nepal. The shopping malls, supermarkets and department stores in the country's capital showcase all kinds of foreign branded goods. Today, from foreign consumer goods to things like Cambridge 'A' level examinations have become accessible to the Nepalese public, or at least to those who can afford them, something that would have been difficult to imagine just a generation ago. The number of Nepalese not only going for foreign employment—over one million, according to one estimate (Seddon et al. 2001: 51)—but also those going to countries like the United States for higher education to the Nepalese academics and intellectuals participating in international conferences and seminars have increased significantly over the years, as Nepal also becomes part of the "global village." The supporters of a globalising "flat" world can point to all these instances as examples of development trickling down to the masses. They may also point out that, as more and more Nepalese go abroad for foreign employment, rural farm labourers as well as urban domestic help have become more expensive. Given that it is the most deprived economically who are unable to go for employment outside, these poorest of the poor have consequently been able to benefit from the increase in wages created by the dearth of manpower inside the country.

The "trickle down" of globalisation cannot, however, hide the glaring inequalities among the different parts of the world, in fact it only highlights them. All data show that as the world has become more and more integrated, the economic disparity between the rich and the poor countries, the haves and the have-nots has also been increasing. The world is "flat" only for the select few, for the rest it remains an unattainable plateau. And it is likely to remain so, with the belief that eventually all parts of the world will benefit equally from "development," from the present technological revolution "a cruel neo-colonial self-deception if ever there was one" (Lyon 2002: 53). The present market globalisation will leave countless many stranded on the other side, like those on the pavement looking wistfully through the bright glass windows of supermarkets and shopping malls at a world they cannot attain. For the many, the "consolation" of globalisation may be that they can work as petrol-pump attendants, supermarket salespersons and as waiters/ waitresses in restaurants.

Market globalisation's attachment to the faster, bigger, taller, its obsession with the new has engendered the conspicuous consumption we are witness to today. The culture of consumerism—if it can be called a culture, which is a moot point—has taken many forms. One manifestation is the South Asian obsession with fair skin, as evidenced in the popular advertisements for "fairness" creams and the like. Another is what has been called the 3 Ms of the Nepalese society, namely money, mobile and motorcycle. Consumerism today has not only become the means through which the upper and middle classes assert their class-*ness*. It is also the medium to fill myriad "empty" lives. Like the Nepalese husband who shows "blue" or pornographic films to his wife to stimulate their sex life, or the husband who, in place of real love and affection, showers his wife with consumer goods in the hope that it will keep her, if not happy, at least quiescent.

Modernity's impact has of course coincided with the West's, i.e. the kernel of modernity own ascendancy all over the world. Its impact, from the crass consumerism of today to that on popular culture and imagination, has been considerable. Which urban educated Nepalese youth, after all, has not attempted to play the guitar, even dreaming of becoming a star *a la* the Beatles, Michael Jackson, Madonna, Eminem and the like? Who has not dreamt of going to the developed countries of the West, especially the United States, for higher studies, for work or even permanent settlement? For the urban upper and middle classes, not only Valentine's Day but also the celebrating of "Happy Birthday" has become an annual ritual, the use in conversation of English words and phrases has become a matter of prestige and the aping of the dress and mannerisms of western popular figures has become a fashion statement. In all this, given its power and position in the world, "Amerika," i.e. the United States has come to acquire a preeminence even among the developed countries of the West. Its visa, not to mention its "green card," has become among the most sought after items for many Nepalese. The "Diversity Visa Program" of the United States every year attracts a significant number of Nepalese eager to go and settle there. The number of Nepalese, which include top Nepalese professionals like doctors, engineers and university teachers to celebrities like film stars and musicians to even parliamentarians, going to the United States in pursuance of the American Dream continues to rise every year. It is not surprising in this context to find that the elites of the Nepalese society like politicians, writers, intellectuals, industrialists, businessmen, etc. either have their grown-up children in the United States or are in the process of sending them there.

Of course, the impact of outside influences on the Nepalese society is not a recent phenomenon, as I have mentioned in Chapter Two. One could, in this context, say that it is the "arc" of the impact and influence that has increased over the years. If in the past north Indian cities from Banaras to Kolkata were the attractions for the Nepalese, today with the improvements in transportation and communication their aspirations have extended much farther. It is the megapolises of the developed world, from Sydney to Tokyo to London to New York, that captivate the Nepalese minds of today. The same could be said of Western fads and fashions. An example in this regard is the English language itself. Although it was by no means as extensive as today, English was popular, not to mention a prestige issue, among the traditional elites of the Nepalese society like the Rana rulers. The Ranas not only inscribed upon the Western style palaces and monuments they built phrases and sentences in the English language, but also gave the women workers working in the palaces names like Rose, Lavender, etc. The use of English was not merely a fad of course, it also served important instrumental ends. Competence in the language was necessary for the Ranas to maintain effective communication with the English-speaking rulers to the south. When the declaration of the emancipation of slaves was read at a public gathering in Kathmandu in 1926, an English version accompanied the Khas-Nepali original. The English version was found necessary to provide clear and first hand information regarding the matter to the British rulers in India (Panday 1987/88: 153, 208-209).

Given that the West's influence throughout the world increased along with its ascendancy, its impact will also no doubt wane with its inevitable decline. The rest of the world that at present looks up, so to say, to the

West will find it a less attractive proposition with the fading of its power and glory. Along with the ebbing of its "hard" power will come the decline in "soft" power, as the world finds the West's ideology, values and way of life less worthy of emulating. In this context, one could well ask whether not only the values that the West has given us, such as liberalism and individual rights, but also such intellectual achievements that modernity has bequeathed us as empirical science will prove to be ephemeral in the long run. Will the world in the future come to regret not only the westernisation but also the modernisation it has undergone at present? Will countries like Nepal and groups like the Nepalese indigenous nationalities come to regret all that is today regarded as progressive and developmental? This question becomes particularly pertinent if we look at the process of Sanskritisation or Hinduisation that groups like the Nepalese indigenous nationalities went through in the past. Nepalese indigenous nationalities today have come to repudiate this Hinduisation, and Sanskritisation no longer remains an attractive ideal for them. They are reverting back to their "original" culture and way of life. Will the same fate befall modernisation and westernisation?

The Modern "Episteme"

The way humans "create" not only values but also knowledge is bound up with the world they experience and live in. Human knowledge does not exist in some ideal realm but is woven into the world of our experiences. Social sciences like economics and political science have also developed with the times. They remain part of the modern experience, a modernity that is associated with concepts like the market and the state. Therefore, just as economics has difficulty conceiving of a world without the market and is market-*ist*, political science is state-*ist*, that is its discourse is centred around the modern concept of the state. A discipline like sociology not only conceives of "societies" of the nation-state, but its concepts like *gemeinschaft* (community) and *gesellschaft* (a society of individuals), from a society of 'status' to 'contract' and 'ascriptive' and 'acquired' values all have the implicit bias of modern societies and against traditional ones. In this context, it is a "fringe" discipline like anthropology that has focused on "pre-modern," "preliterate" societies. Anthropology and anthropologists have done much to destabilise the foundational civilised/primitive dichotomy, thus helping to dethrone the privileged status of Western knowledge.

The question remains: will, with the eclipse of the West, all its achievements, including empirical science and knowledge, i.e. the epistemological "baggage" associated with the West also fade from the collective memory of humankind? After all, it is not the "will to knowledge" *per se* that drives human societies but rather the "will to power," or the basic instinct of survival to cope with an alien environment. Also, after the horrors of the twentieth century, the threat of nuclear catastrophe, environmental disaster, etc., it is no longer "fashionable" to have unbounded faith in human reason. Modern knowledge promised to free humanity from bondage, but instead went on to impose its own tyrannies. Modernity can be accused of not only colonialism, racism and sexism, but the knowledge it generated has been used to justify all kinds of inequalities and injustices.

Given all this, should the solution to our present problems be sought in pre-modern, i.e. religious alternatives, as some have suggested (Lyon 2002)? This would of course be quite in accordance with the revivalist practices evident all around the world, including in Nepal. Followers of various religious faiths would no doubt be quick to point out that the answers to the world's problems can be found in religion, in particular in their own religion. The "book" of their own religion, i.e. the *Bible, Gita, Koran, Tripitak*, etc. has the key to the world's ills, and one need not look any further. The values of their religion should pervade all walks of life, and religious strictures should guide everyday conduct. As a banner during an Easter procession by Christians in Kathmandu read 'Religiosity makes a nation strong,' the followers of various faiths would no doubt wish to see their own religion hold sway in society, arguing that it is religion that holds the fabric of the society together and strengthens it.

The malaise of modernity, the crisis faced by it has not unsurprisingly brought forth various comments and reactions. In a persuasively argued book John Horgan makes the claim that science, pure science is coming to an end (Horgan 1997). Science, itself a product of modernity and among the—if not the—noblest manifestation of the human quest for knowledge, has become a victim of its own success. There is nothing left to discover, as the various fields of science, from chemistry to physics, from biology to astronomy, reach the limits of human cognition and comprehension. Given this, the science practiced by some of today's most celebrated scientists such as Stephen Hawking is not science at all but post-empirical (another post!) science, that is it is a science that cannot be empirically tested and verified at all. With their talk of "time travel," "wormholes" and "baby universe," it is not empirical but post-empirical or ironic science. It is more like poetry, literature or even medieval religion than the "hard" science bequeathed to us by modernity.

Of course, as I pointed out at the beginning of this chapter, there is no denying the "provisional" nature of all scientific theories and discoveries. The certitude and definitiveness to science that we are taught in schools often obscures this. It also tends to obscure the competing theories that exist within the fields of science. Moreover, the supremacy accorded to science epistemologically means that it imposes its own homogeneity, obliterating diverse and opposing viewpoints and perspectives. This leads to the dichotomies we see today, not only of civilised/primitive but also of scientific/non-scientific or mythical, modern/traditional, urban/rural, written/oral, industrial/agricultural, with the latter seen as lowly, even wrong. But I would like to repeat the question: will, with the eclipse of the West, all the "episteme" of modern science also be consigned to oblivion, discarded like the proverbial baby with the bathwater? And should we again start believing that women can be witches, or that earthquakes occur because of some serpent living in the earth moving its body, or that, as some Nepalese intellectuals have stated, humans were created on the top of Mount Everest?

Although there cannot be any compromises vis-à-vis the issue of recognising and respecting the world's diversity and plurality, there does nonetheless seem a limit to accepting all the superstitions and practices associated with this cultural heterogeneity. As Tariq Ali, defending the values of the Enlightenment, asks: who would imagine that religions have become less of an illusion since the days of the Enlightenment? The Enlightenment attacked religion for two reasons, because it was a set of ideological delusions and because it was a system of institutional oppression, with immense powers of persecution and intolerance. Why, then, should we today abstain from religious criticism and why should we abandon either of these legacies today (Ali 2003: 337)? Religions, one could argue, have hardly become less of an "ideological delusion" today than in the past. A Sri Lankan Buddhist talking to the BBC following the December 26, 2004 tsunami declared that the tsunami was the result of the killings of animals that Christians had undertaken during Christmas Day. The Buddhist apparently thought the Boxing Day tsunami and the devastation it had wrought as an appropriate reaction for the "sins" of the previous day. On the other hand, some Christians in Nepal opposed the sacrificing of animals by Hindus during the Hindu festival of Dashain, arguing that Jesus had already given his life and sacrificed himself (*Kantipur* 2008: 2). A much publicised recent case related to religion in Nepal is that of a Buddhist youth meditating in the forests of central tarai. The youth, dubbed as an incarnation of Buddha himself, was reported by the media to have meditated for eight months without partaking of even water and food or engaging in bodily functions like urinating and defecating. In this context, one can also point to the case of Mother Teresa and her "beatification" and elevation to "sainthood" following the Catholic Church's claim of her performing a "miracle." Despite her life of uncommon sacrifice, the "miracle," according to the Church, comprises of Mother Teresa curing a physically ill person of his or her ailment by just touching the concerned person.

The West "outgrew" medieval religion—in this case Christianity—through centuries of historical incidents and accidents. The Lisbon earthquake on All Saints Day of 1755 that led to massive deaths and destruction is said to have shaken the European intellectuals' belief in a benevolent deity. The upheavals the West went through led to deicides as well as regicides, not surprisingly given that kings were regarded as the representatives of god on earth. The centuries of ferment the West underwent engendered the uniquely modern worldview, which owing to its special circumstances has today become worldwide. This modern worldview with its emphasis on reason has brought forth its own reactions. To classify is to comprehend, but human reason's penchant for classification means that much of reality is left out in the process. In the name of simplicity of comprehension, we miss out on so much of the existing reality. As the philosopher Jacques Derrida pointed out, in the process of creating something, something else inevitably gets left out. These exclusive structures can become repressive, and that repression comes with consequences. What is repressed does not disappear but always returns to unsettle every construction, no matter how secure that construction seems (Taylor 2004: 5).

The human tendency to classify, comprehend and ultimately control is of course manifested in the modern nation-state itself. Nation-states remain as the supreme embodiments of the exclusive structures created by the modern mind. The tendency to see the world in straight lines also finds manifestation in doctrines and philosophies like that of the so-called scientific socialism. Thus, with remarkable exactitude, Mao could say that Stalin was 70 percent right and 30 percent wrong, while Deng Xiaoping and his heirs in China could say of Mao himself that Mao was 70 percent right and 30 percent wrong.*

---

* The scientific pretensions of Communism have often contrasted with the more "primordial" sentiments among its adherents and followers. There is the saying that Mao "sinified" Marxism, and also the mention of the influence on Mao of Chinese culture, thought and literature, of Confucious thought and of the Chinese concept of *yin* and *yang*. Likewise, Vietnamese communists have talked about the "4000 years of the history of the Vietnamese nation." And Russian communists, during World War II, had to take recourse to national sentiments to

Nevertheless, science, modern natural science has succeeded in giving us incomparable insights into nature, into the wonder and the mystery of the world we live in and the universe we inhabit. These insights include Isaac Newton's theory of gravity, Albert Einstein's theory of relativity and Charles Darwin's theory of evolution by natural selection, "the single best idea anyone has ever had" according to the philosopher Daniel Dennet. Despite the relativity or provisionality of all science, these scientific theories may never ever be bettered upon, may well prove to be irreplaceable. Unlike the "anti-science philosopher" Paul Feyerabend, I tend to believe that scientific theories like these may prove to be true even after a couple of hundred years, or after a thousand years. Modern science and its achievements remain not inconsiderable, this despite the fact that science can be—and has been—misused, or that science imposes its own homogeneity upon the world.

Science has been successful in not only explaining the world, but its discoveries have also led to technological innovations of widespread applicability. Like the spread of fire in remote past, societies all over the world have been eager to benefit from the fruits of science. Science is an integral part of the educational curriculum in schools and colleges,

---

mobilise the people for the war. They talked about the Russia of the Czars and of the past and the Russian fatherland that had to be defended against external invaders. There is, in this context, also the "macabre" spectacle of the Lenin Mausoleum in Communist Soviet Union, followed by similar monuments for Mao, Ho Chi Minh and Kim Il Sung in Communist China, Vietnam and North Korea respectively. Not only was the church rehabilitated in Soviet Russia for reasons of expediency, but the Lenin Mausoleum that had been set up, according to a Marxist writer, despite the protests of Lenin's wife and widow and members of the Communist Party central committee, was to become a place of pilgrimage and fascination for the people. This monument to "primitive magic" erected in the very heart of the Russian Revolution was, to old Bolsheviks, "an insult to their dignity, and—so they thought—an insult to the maturity of the Soviet people." The mausoleum was "the totem pole" and the shrine of Stalinism, and Stalin's oath of fealty to the dead Lenin had all the undertones of a funeral homage to a dead tribal chief" (Deutscher 1984: 115).

and science has set its own standards regarding the way we perceive the world. (In this context, it is interesting to note not only the scientific pretensions of ideologies like Marxism, but also of religions like Buddhism and Hinduism, teachers and followers of which have often made claims about the "scientificity" of their faiths.) As a method of inquiry into nature, science, not entirely unjustifiably, has been successful in acquiring epistemological precedence over all other knowledge systems. I say not entirely unjustifiably because science appears as a fundamental break from the past just as the advent of agriculture or the onset of industrialisation was during the course of human history. It is difficult today to imagine any present or future human society existing without science. Like the human course-altering innovations of the past, science, too, aspires to be universal.

An Interconnected World

The increasing interconnectedness among the peoples of the world has led to some shared practices, even if for purely instrumental purposes. One could cite as examples in this regard the Arabic numeral for counting, the Gregorian calendar for keeping time or even English as an "international" language for wider communication. Some unity in diversity has to be sought simply for human intercourse and interaction to be possible. This is a paradox similar to that one faced by deconstructionists. Deconstructionists see language as eternal "play," the 'perpetual sliding of the signified over the signifier,' but they, too, have to rely on the communicative power of language to say determinate things and to express themselves clearly and forcefully (Abrams 1988). To say that there are infinite ways in which language games can be played one has to be able to use language with clarity so that others can comprehend what exactly one is saying. Despite the postmodernists' insistence on *jouissance* or play, humans nonetheless have a tendency to impose order and stability to a reality that is by nature disorderly, unstable and chaotic. No one, after all, finds it easy to live uncomplainingly and fearlessly with the thesis that human reality is constantly being made and unmade, and that anything like a stable essence is constantly under threat. We all need some foundation on which to stand. The question is how extreme and unchangeable is our formulation of what this foundation is. In spite of the distraction and a great many vague desires, impulses and images, the human mind seems persistently to formulate what the anthropologist Claude Levi-Strauss has called a science of the concrete. A "primitive" tribe, for example, assigns a definite place, function and significance to every leafy species in its immediate environment (Said 1995: 53, 333).

The construction of foundations, a centre leads, of course, to exclusion, marginalisation, stereotyping and much worse. The erection of a standard means that anything and anyone not conforming to it are seen as deviant and wrong. Despite all the talk of "end of ideology," there are powerful "isms" or "paradigms" that continue to drive human society, especially in a developing country like Nepal. The first and foremost is obviously nationalism. To say that someone is anti-national, separatist or splittist is among the worst abuses that can be hurled against anyone in the Nepalese society (similar to the one against those who oppose development). A political party like the Unified Communist Party of Nepal (Maoist), while even going to the extent of promising "self-determination rights" to various peoples, has also been among the most strident champions of Nepalese nationalism, railing against what it calls imperialist and expansionist forces. If the contradiction inherent in their position has escaped the Maoists, the nationalist rhetoric employed by its leaders (and also by leaders of other political parties) has nonetheless been a surefire way to mobilise the people, garner votes and incite public opinion. In this context, it may, ironically, be the political forces that have raised secessionist and separatist slogans and called for outright independence from the Nepalese state that may lead to a redefinition of Nepalese nationalism.

Another powerful ideology in today's Nepalese context is development. It is this enticing "fruit" of development that has led to the current situation in Kathmandu. Otherwise, how can one justify the inordinate expansion, the "concrete jungle," given that experts have raised fears that the extracting of groundwater to serve the needs of the growing Kathmandu Valley denizens may well lead to the caving in of the Valley floor? (That the best solution to Kathmandu's water as well as environmental woes is to simply shift the capital from Kathmandu will no doubt be contentious and opposed by Kathmandu-ites themselves, such is the allure of development.) The ideology of progress and development remain as powerful motivating forces, although recently another "ism," namely environmentalism has slowly emerged to challenge the discourse of development. Going "green" is an often heard of slogan these days globally, to which the Nepalese government has given heed to some extent by establishing the Ministry of Environment.

The "ideology" of environmentalism has come to challenge one of the most cherished ideals of modernity, that of the idea of progress. The exploiting of nature through human ingenuity to fulfill all human wants, the concept of limitless growth and development and of technological innovations to overcome all obstacles in the process, all these ideas are being challenged by an emerging environmentalism. The one planet we inhabit and its finite natural resources cannot sustain the modern human's craving for infinite development, hence the stress on "greener" alternative solutions. Nevertheless, the idea of development as such remains so powerful paradigmatically still that there is considerable ambivalence vis-à-vis these solutions. After all, how to convince a "deprived" citizen of a developing country like Nepal that he or she will not be able to even at some time in the future acquire the material affluence that the citizens of western developed countries at present enjoy, even take for granted? Given the enticements of the bright lights of the developed West, the pleading for environmental "sanity" to development may well fall on deaf years. The making by an Indian automaker of a $2500 car accessible to the "common" people of India can be illustrative in this regard. The achievement should be a cause for celebration or of concern is open to question, given the environmental consequences of the over a billion population of India all aspiring to a car in their homes (Friedman 2007: 5).

The "lack" or "inadequacy" non-Western peoples perceive vis-à-vis their own societies in comparison to the developed West has of course been engendered and exacerbated by the paternalistic and openly condescending attitude that the West has traditionally had towards non-Western societies and peoples. Like the Rana Prime Minister Jang Bahadur publicly berated during his visit to Britain in the mid-nineteenth century for not being punctual, non-Western peoples have often been made painfully aware of their supposed foibles and shortcomings. The stereotyping of non-Western ways of life has meant that non-Western societies and peoples have been quick to conform than to invite ridicule. Even the "powerful" Chinese government, along with discouraging activities like picking one's nose and spitting in public, went to the extent of the banning of the sale of dog meat in Beijing for the duration of the Olympic Games held in the city in 2008. (As regards the Nepalese context, although Nepalese even today are not exactly the epitome of punctuality—as is implied by the adage 'Nepali time'—they are nonetheless more aware about the significance of "clock-time" than in the nineteenth century. Not only has the wearing of watches proliferated, but there is also the 'fashion' of building clock-towers in townships around the country.)

Globalisation, as I have mentioned previously, would have that non-Western societies and peoples ameliorate their "lack" by becoming more and more like the developed societies of the West. They become, if not westernised, at least modernised. They learn the skills, norms, values and way of life of modern societies. Unlike the Mughal emperor Akbar who turned a Guttenberg printing press gifted to him into scrap-metal by letting it lie idle and unused (Gyawali 2006: 73), they adapt to the technological innovations of modernity. The shining beacon of a civilised West will thus illuminate the darkest corners of the world and its peoples. And modernity will bring all of us to the shining city on the hill. Some may even point as evidence of this dazzling vision to the "branded" department stores, shopping malls and supermarkets, as well as the private banks, in Kathmandu, with their gleaming marble floors and glass windows, which may make you feel that you are in any developed country in the West.

After the then King Gyanendra usurped power from the parliamentary political parties on October 4, 2002 by sacking the elected Prime Minister, the ensuing confrontation between the King and the political parties was likened by some Nepalese observers to the conflict between the King and the parliament in Britain in the centuries gone by. In this scheme of things, the trajectory of development to be followed by developing societies like Nepal is the one already undergone by the developed West. And if there any anomalies, like that newspapers in Nepal, including the broadsheet dailies, cease publication during the Hindu festivals of Dashain and Tihar or that you may not get fresh bread in the market on Saturday because bakeries remain closed for the weekend holiday, these are minor hindrances that will be "smoothened" along the way.

Thus, a developing country like Nepal is to make the transition from a traditional "exploitative," "predatory" state to a modern "welfare" state. According to the stages of development conceived by modernity, an urban Nepalese youth a generation ago aspired to possess a bicycle, including a "fancy" Chinese made one, now his or her preferred mode of transport is the motorcycle and a generation hence he or she will have graduated to be the proud owner of a car. The discourse of development would have us believe that there is an inevitability, even logic, to the process. But, as I have argued, there is nothing inevitable or logical about it. It is only the "paradigm" of progress and development that beguiles us into thinking so. The future remains an enlightened guesswork at best. Marxism, invoking a "dubious iron law" of society, had predicted that capitalism would make the evolutionary transition to communism. The twentieth century remains as testimony to the mismatch between the prediction and the reality, a mismatch for which thousands, even millions, of people were made to pay with their lives. For a future that was never to come, countless peoples in countless countries around the world had to sacrifice their only present.

Modernity's vision of a future based on continuous progress and development, of "brave new worlds," has instead led to dystopias, Orwellian as well as otherwise. The sociologist Max Weber had prophesied that the future would be an iron prison of reason and bureaucracy. Reason, supposed to lead to human freedom, instead went on to "clip freedom's wings." Certainly, our cities that are "noisier" and "nastier" hardly inspire hope in the future. In one of his novels, the science fiction writer Isaac Asimov foresaw humanity living in large isolated "estates" avoiding all kinds of physical contact with each other. The denizens of the sparsely populated planet of Solaris only "see" each other through three-dimensional images, considering physical proximity to be abhorrent. (The Solarians have a robot based economy, with almost every task performed by robots.) The Solarians do not have any knowledge of their offspring nor do the children, who are brought up collectively, know who their parents are (Asimov 1960). Thus, human society is deprived of some of the most fundamental institutions that we today take for granted, namely family and marriage. In this context, one can only speculate about what tomorrow has in store for us. The playwright George Bernard Shaw has written that humans in the future will loose interest in what appears to us as such a fundamental biological need as sex. Today, the advances in science and technology have even raised the spectre of genetically modified "post-humanity human beings."

All the challenges we face today, from the paradox of universalism to identity politics, from development fatigue to unequal development, from climate change to nuclear, biological and chemical weapons, from consumption that has no end to meaninglessness, all point to the malaise of modernity. One may, in this context, dispute whether the term postmodern (as well as the numerous other 'posts') appropriately signifies our present condition, but there is no mistaking the sense of a 'break' from a past of the last couple of centuries. The era of Western domination, not only militarily but also intellectually and culturally, is coming to an end. This raises new challenges, epistemic as well as moral. It calls for a new "paradigm," a new way of looking at things and seeking answers to questions. These answers may well take us into totally uncharted waters, as the advances in genetics and cloning make clear. Genetic modification raises the possibility of even the redefinition of humanity, of what it means to be human (post-humanity!).

7

A World in Transition: Rethinking the Present

In keeping with the current usage of *posts*, we might say that the world today is post-Western. This is not to deny the considerable influence the West continues to exert on the rest of the world. The events in the West have implications for the rest of the world, from the fall of the Berlin Wall to the recent "colour" revolutions in the countries of eastern Europe. The West can appear as a "trend-setter," as "iconic": thus the tri-colour, following the French Revolution, has become the national flag of numerous countries around the world. Today, the events and images beamed via television mean that they can be copied and imitated by people around the world. During the recent movement in the country against the autocratic rule of the King, the agitating crowds were seen offering flowers to police personnel in a clear reference to the events in eastern Europe. In this context, Nepalese can celebrate, even shed tears, at Barack Obama's victory as the President of the United States. The "aping" of the West can of course be contentious, one can point here to the use, in place of traditional toilets, of the "water intensive" commodes in a place like Kathmandu with its acute shortage of water (not to mention the use of toilet paper!). Like the Nepalese youth ploughing the field in some remote part of the country wearing Levis and using medieval technology, non-Western societies like Nepal are, so to say, caught between two worlds. The recent assertiveness also means that they are increasingly "talking back" to the West, hence the use of the term post-Western.

So, what will the post-Western world look like? Well, for one, it will be heterogeneous, with diverse, not to mention divergent, perspectives, viewpoints, opinions and interests. A well known Nepalese indigenous nationality poet and academician talks about the two "stages" of poetry writing. In the first stage, the poets and the poetry of disadvantaged and marginalised groups are representative of the particular group, language and culture as a whole. Given that it is the period of awakening and the raising of awareness, the poets and their poetry carry the burden of the entire community. But this does not remain forever, and literature has to represent one's "innermost feelings." After going from the first stage to the second stage, poets and writers begin to express their gravest and most serious thoughts artistically (Bairagi Kaila, quoted in NEFEN 2003/04: 30).

The above comment is not only in keeping with modernity's conception of the stages of development, but also suffers from the same flaw. By ascribing to the universal a superior status, it denigrates what it deems as "particular" as lowly, thus marginalising it. From this it is but just one step to homogenisation and stereotyping and assimilation and the destroying of diversity. Instead of such a position, a future that takes into account the interconnectivity of the present world while at the same time respecting diversity and local aspirations appears more plausible, not to mention just. As Peter Drucker has said, the more transnational the world becomes, the more "tribal" it will also be. Tomorrow's educated person will have to be prepared for life in a global world. It will be a "Westernised" world, but also increasingly a "tribalised" world. The educated person must become a "citizen of the world"—in vision, horizon, information. But he or she will also have to draw nourishment from their local roots and, in turn, enrich and nourish their own culture (Drucker 1994: 155, 215). Thus, the world will not only be suitably modern but also selectively modern, as the diverse peoples around the world bring their own rich and varied experiences in their encounter with modernity. The neologism 'glocal' quite aptly captures this situation.

Seeking Some Common Ground

As the world becomes more diverse, indeed celebrates its diversity, what are the commonalities and shared values that can, if not unite, at least make civilised interaction among these diverse peoples possible?

After all, as the world becomes more and more interconnected, there is the urgent need to find issues that we can all agree upon as human beings. (As David Harvey, pointing to "one of the great ironies of the period," says, a world war became possible only after the world had become so highly united [Harvey 1989: 278].) The Enlightenment humanism and its universalising and utopian spirit is not, as we have seen, without its contradictions. Given this, it may be difficult to agree with the view that there is today an international civil society (Walzer 1995: 3). Cynics may well say that instead, in a world with the minority rich and the majority poor, it might more appropriately be called the "Davos Culture" (Huntington 1996: 57).

Davos in Switzerland is the place where every year about a thousand businessmen, bankers, government officials, intellectuals and journalists from scores of countries around the world meet for the World Economic Forum. Almost all these people hold university degrees in the physical sciences, social sciences, business or law, work with words and/or numbers, are reasonably fluent in English, are employed by governments, corporations and academic institutions with extensive international involvements, and travel frequently outside their own country. They generally share beliefs in individualism, market economies and political democracy, which are also common among people in the West. The Davos people control virtually all international institutions, many of the world's governments and the bulk of the world's economic and military capabilities. The Davos Culture, hence, is tremendously important. Nonetheless, outside of the West, the culture is probably shared by less than 50 million people or around one percent of the world's population and perhaps by as few as one-tenth of one percent of the world's population. The elites or leaders who share in the Davos Culture do not necessarily have a secure grip on power in their own societies. The common intellectual culture exists only at the elite level. Its roots are shallow in many societies and it is doubtful whether, even at the diplomatic level, it embraces what is called a common moral culture or set of common values, as distinct from a common intellectual culture (Ibid.: 57-58). Also, the elites may be sanguine about disenfranchisement, particularly those employed directly by transnational companies. As they become ever more linked to the global economy, they have less of a stake in the performance and potential of their less fortunate compatriots. The transnational company executive operates increasingly on a global basis. He shares the social and political values of the international business community. He may move effortlessly from country to country, as the demands of his company dictate. Speaking, perhaps, a second language, and conversant at the very least with the terms on foreign-language menus, he feels more comfortable in other countries than the common men and women (Horsman and Marshall 1995: 226). The gap between the elites and others becomes evident from the comment of an observer that the ordinary Nepalese, if they came to know about the exorbitant salaries of foreign development specialists and consultants, might well have a heart attack (Dixit 2006: 359). The Nepalese observer was referring to foreigners working in Nepal, but his comment remains apt for Nepalese elites, i.e. intellectual-consultants as well.

Nevertheless, in an increasingly interconnected world, there have to be some basic norms and practices, the "thin" morality to which all of us can aspire and follow. One may or may not believe in an "international civil society," but there has to be consensus regarding some basic issues of civility and decency, even if for the simple reason that failure to do so can invite horrendous consequences. Thomas S. Kuhn, in his "seminal postmodern text," had pointed out that although there are some fields of science that remain in a state of constant flux and go from one "paradigm" to another, there are nevertheless some fields that converge on a "paradigm," that achieve consensus or "normalcy." Likewise, we, too, are tempted to strive for some common ground, to seek for "normalcy" amidst a reality that is always in a state of constant change, of flux. This is the "paradigm" of our times, to guide us in our thoughts and actions.

Writing about multiculturalism and the politics of recognition, Charles Taylor wondered if members of groups are publicly identified with the dominant characteristics, practices and values of their group, whether our particular identities will take public precedence over our more universal identity as persons, deserving of mutual respect, civil and political liberties and decent life chances, simply by virtue of our equal and common humanity (Taylor 1994: 9). In today's world the idea of basic shared decency and civility is not mere idealism but an urgent necessity. In this context, Michael Walzer has spoken of a "minimalist universalism" that condemns practices like ethnic cleansing and genocide but that does not enjoin the more culturally specific standards of Western rights-liberalism or even of the Universal Declaration of Human Rights (quoted in Walker 1997: 184). The idea of a decent minimalism could be expanded in a positive direction as well, recognising such generic virtues as humanness, sexual responsibility, the sustenance of marriage and family, and a manageable material basis of human life. In a multicultural world, this minimalism will guide us in our efforts to build understanding, tolerance and respect among diverse groups of peoples.

What can be the basis for this minimalism? The first is obviously the acknowledgement that, contrary to what instrumental reason says, there are varied ways of living one's life equally justifiable and valid and "good." Hence, even such epochal events during the course of human history as agriculture and industrialisation need not be regarded as universal applicable to all times and places. Although we have the tendency to think of our own way of doing things, our own time and place as "universal" and "correct," it is obviously not so. It is just one particular human experience amidst the myriad of experiences. Among these experiences, there are those with purely functional value. In the modern world of "office time," there is obviously a virtue in being punctual and on time. The leisurely pace of rural life is simply incompatible with the modern experience. The same can be said of cleanliness and the disposal of bodily waste.

In modern mass societies there is obviously the need for disposing waste matter in an efficient manner, simply for the reason of hygiene. In crowded modern towns and cities, even the act of spitting can be a hazardous activity, because you may well spit on another person. The modern obsession with cleanliness, one could therefore argue, may even have an "evolutionary" purpose. (This despite the fact that some seem intent on being exceptions, as is evinced by the comment of a former Maoist minister that he took a bath once a month [*Himal Khabarpatrika* 2008: 19]!)

The close proximity in which we live the modern life means that it has engendered its own codes of conduct, its own standards of behaviour. This leads to the uniformity of behaviour of modern societies, as for instance in the case of "table manners." (On the other hand, I know of individuals in the traditional Nepalese society who do not consider farting while eating to be unseemly conduct.) The "mass produced" standardisation of modern societies with its emphasis on uniformity and homogeneity and claims to universality is, nonetheless, destructive of the world's diversity. Nepalese economists have pointed to the "dualistic" nature of the Nepalese economy. On the one hand, there is the affluent section of the population in urban pockets indulging in "vulgar" display of wealth and ostentatious consumption while, on the other, there is the vast rural hinterland where money and market have barely penetrated (Shrestha 2002). Modernity and modernisation theorists would no doubt say that the latter has to be brought under the sway of the market and the money economy for its own good. This is development, this is the way the "Pakhe" are brought under the civilising influence of modernity. This is how the great juggernaut of development brings all of humanity to the hoped for utopia. But development, as I have already mentioned, today faces its own challenges. Without the guarantee that it will be either sustainable or equitable, even fervent enthusiasts can have difficulty convincing themselves that it is worthwhile foregoing their distinct identities to assimilate into the so-called development mainstream. (In this context, just like the ambivalence over the world's "cheapest" car made in India, it is worth wondering whether another "developing" country, namely China will come to regret its own obsession with cars. A generation ago China was renowned for its bicycles as the popular means of transport. Today, development has meant that for the millions of upwardly mobile Chinese cars have become the things to aspire for, replacing the bicycle. This is leading to environmental consequences in the world's most populous country of an unprecedented scale. In our own "developing" country Nepal, cars are said to have become not a luxury but a necessity not only for the upper classes but also for the urban middle classes.)

The "Open-Ended" Modern World

Although developmental modernity and the 'Nepalisation' project of Nepalese nationalism have both strove to assimilate diverse peoples under one metanarrative, they are nonetheless significant differences between the two. Apart from the contradiction that while modernity aspires to be universal and nationalism, one of the products of modernity, is particularistic, national sentiments have often run contrary to modern aspirations. Thus, the Nepalese state, while claiming to be a modern nation-state, could also give continuity to the traditional values of the ruling Hindu "high" caste groups of the Nepalese society. Indeed, the modern nation-state became the means for the propagation of Hindu norms and values throughout the society. The Nepalese state assimilated the diverse peoples of the Nepalese society around the Hindu norms and values of the ruling caste groups of the Nepalese society. Today, the oppressed groups of the Nepalese society are claiming the right 'to be different' and 'to remain different.' Although cultures are permeable and are not obviously self-contained entities, the failure to distinguish different groups and cultures can nonetheless lead to assimilation in a roundabout way. This is best exemplified in the South Asian context by the Hindu religion, where an over-inclusive and over-elastic definition of Hinduism means that

Hinduism is invoked both as a supreme assimilative power and a practice of ingesting diverse traditions and sects. Given this, all past religious differences and dissent are seen as differences and dissent from within—tribals as incomplete Hindus, Buddhists and Sikhs as breakaway Hindus who can be intermittently incorporated, etc. (Sangari 1999). In this context, anyone and anything can be said to be Hindu.

Today, the self-confidence, if not assertiveness, among groups like the Nepalese indigenous nationalities vis-à-vis their identities has manifested in activities like 'writing' themselves. The activities of indigenous nationalities are aimed at ameliorating the 'lack' they have been made to feel by the modern world. It is a world that is in many ways fundamentally different from what they have lived and experienced. As J.G.A. Pocock, referring to the Maori indigenous peoples, says,

> The time structure of the Maori world was mythic, composed of ancestral and cosmic images. But the movement of property from possession to alienability entailed a history more drastic than any of the stadial sequences designed to precede it; a process of commodification in which all goods become mobile and *homo* became *mercator*, committed to exchange. As goods became commodities, exchange transformed their use and character. The future became open, at the price of uncertainty. Maori, accustomed to living in a cosmos of reciprocity, justice and revenge, found themselves in a process of shifting patterns, in which the new must be undertaken without seeing its outcome, nothing was quite what it seemed....This is life in the open-endedness of history, a vision of things frighteningly necessary to the open society in which humans seek freedom and self-determination. Neo-conservative historians sometimes point out that even the most barbarous and brutal Europeans encountered

> by Maori knew things about living in a history of differences, and therefore about being free, unknowable in a closed Maori cosmos that taught no response to them, and that once the sailors had arrived, freedom could only be had by living in a history like—if not identical with—theirs (Pocock 2000: 30-31).

The "new" world is life in the open-endedness of history, a history that is quite unlike their own. Democracy itself is based on the epistemological premise that there is no final truth about what is good for society, belonging to the domain of revelation or special knowledge, and that the only criterion for the public good is what the people, freely organised, will choose, not what some expert or prophet decrees on the basis of superior knowledge. The anti-paternalism of democracy is here the direct descendant of the anti-paternalism of liberalism and rests on the same epistemological foundation (Beetham 1993: 57).

The modern world is a world with complex roles and permeable status hierarchies. Thus, a "waiter" in the United States can go on to become the Secretary of State. For traditional peoples accustomed to living within a "closed" future, where the place of work (the field) often was an extension of the place of residence (the home), the changed state of affairs of the modern world can be confusing, not to mention deeply unsettling. It calls for fundamental behavioural changes, from the "personal trust" of family, kin, tribe of pre-modern societies, with the "hostile stranger/outsider" to the "impersonal trust" of modern societies and "where there is no stranger/outsider," from the "face to face trust versus universal rights for strangers." Given this, it is not surprising that Nepalese have been regarded as "cold." Even educated Nepalese, in their desperate aping of the American way of life, though they may say 'Hi' to their near and dear ones, will not however say 'Hi' to total strangers. (It is worth remembering here that in the medieval

European society the stranger, along with orphans and widows, formed the most vulnerable sections of the society.)*

The modern world where "acquired" values take precedence over "ascriptive" ones is a society supposedly of "individuals." In its extreme manifestation, as described in Isaac Asimov's novel, the individual is shorn of all particularities like family, kin and other such relationships to be tied in "impersonal trust" with other "individuals." The emphasis on individuality means that in modern societies the traditional extended family has given way to the nuclear family. This despite the fact that with the husband and wife both working outside the home nowadays, the grandparents in the family could perform the very useful function of looking after the growing children. Also—and this is especially important with regard to groups like the indigenous nationalities—the

---

* If we believe in the modern idea of progress and development, some comparisons might well be in order here. It has been said that not much more than a century ago, the average European was an illiterate villager who never went beyond walking distance from the village, from birth to death, and who had little idea of what was happening outside it. It was not the power of an idea that urbanised and educated the Western masses and put them in touch with the whole world, but the proliferation, within the economic sphere, of innovations in transportation, communication and production that enabled, and indeed compelled, the Western masses to exchange the "darkness" of village life for the "lights" of the city (Rosenberg and Birdzel, Jr. 1987: 265).

In this context, there are inhabitants of villages like *Khokana* adjoining the capital Kathmandu in Nepal who even today have never travelled outside their own village. Of course, the conditions that existed just a century ago in the "developed" West can be gleaned from any of Charles Dickens's novels, with their portrayal of dirt, grime, crime and general life of squalor and poverty. In this context, Nepalese—especially the denizens of urban centres like Kathmandu—may take vicarious satisfaction from the fact that in the nineteenth century the stench from the River Thames in London at times became so unbearable that it led to the halting of the proceedings of the House of Commons at Westminster. There has also been mention of a great London "smog" killing an estimated 700 people with respiratory problems in one single week of December 1873 (Kennedy 1994: 96).

elderly grandparents could pass on the traditional culture of the group, for instance the language, to their grandchildren.

As modernity breaks down traditions, the new is adopted almost for the sake of the new. The equating of old age, even the appearance of grey hair, with wisdom of traditional societies is replaced by the youthful vigour and "dynamism" of modern ones. For the modern mind, it may be difficult to believe that in Nepal individuals who began their political career in the 1940s still hold centerstage in the politics of the country. In a traditional society, youth is not only regarded as synonymous with inexperience but also with the absence of intelligence and wisdom. Hence, it is not uncommon still in the Nepalese society to hear grown-ups berating youthful "upstarts" for being "too clever or smart." (The difference between the traditional and the modern is perhaps well illustrated if we compare Nepalese Prime Ministers with the current American President. The latter is a youthful looking "hunk." By contrast, Nepalese Prime Ministers have often appeared as patriarchs, elderly figures "wisened" by years of experience. This is true also of the recently resigned Maoist Prime Minister who, despite being just a couple of years older than the American President and despite being the head of what he likes to call a "revolutionary" and "fundamentally transformatory" communist party, is a grandfatherly figure with a paunch.)

As modernisation continues apace, societies and peoples come forth with their own strategies to cope with it. Like everything else, modernity creates its own ideology justifying itself. The first and foremost of these ideologies is obviously the belief in the desirability and the inevitability of progress. Although past civilisations also sought to maximise comfort for themselves—indeed the 'C' of civilisation can also be said to stand for comfort, with civilisation and comfort being almost synonymous—the belief that this state of affairs can continue forever is an uniquely modern phenomenon. This belief in untrammelled progress is what makes us bear whatever modernity throws at us. The fact that our children are no longer what they used to be due to the "new" phenomenon of teenage-*ness*, the fact that our obsession with material wealth and consumption need not enhance our quality of life and happiness, the fact that our sedentary modern lifestyle is fundamentally unhealthy and we have to "waste" some time everyday in the gym, morning walks and the like, all these, and many more, become bearable only as long as we continue believing that our "tomorrows" will not only be markedly different from but also somehow, in some way better than our "todays." Once we cease doing so—indeed, this is what explains the phenomenon of postmodernity—modernity loses much of its lustre. Today's revivalist practices, the emphasis on one's culture and one's roots, identity politics are not therefore, as some have suggested, "illusions" created by capitalism, or the propagation of Western developed countries and their non-governmental organisations, but point to something deeper, i.e. the malaise of modernity. If tomorrow need not be "better"—and there is, after all, no guarantee that it will be—then why not value and cherish our present, or even the past?

And a Multicultural World

Given this, the attempt to build understanding among different groups and cultures becomes even more of an urgent necessity. The emphasis on multiculturalism, a multicultural world is not merely a fad, a fashion but a matter of principle. The diversity of the world is not an irritant to be eliminated but a source of strength to be celebrated. To those who have pointed to the "dualistic" nature of the Nepalese economy as if it is something of a "lack" or an "inadequacy" to be ameliorated, we say that may not only the economy but also the world long remain not only dualistic but also pluralistic! Cultures and ways of life are not merely embellishments but have instrumental purposes, and in different circumstances different cultures and ways of life can have their usefulness. Modernity with its claims to universality is antagonistic of this and, hence, remains flawed, wrong.

Nevertheless, modernity continues to remain a powerful force of our times, and its achievements remain not inconsiderable. Maybe modernity's confidence in human reason to solve all problems and ameliorate all ills was misplaced. Maybe it was wrong to think that "this one-day fly, this little bit of nothing, a human being—according to today's cosmology!—can figure it all out" (Paul Feyerabend, quoted in Horgan 1997: 54). But we only have to look at the other side, to all the "medievalism being peddled in the garb of identity" to realise that modernity cannot be denounced *in toto*. A well known Nepalese anthropologist created controversy with the publication of his book in which he squarely blamed Nepal's lack of progress and development on the "fatalistic" attitude of the Nepalese (Bista 1991). In the traditional Nepalese society, it is not uncommon to believe that everything happens according to one's fate, as it is "written" in one's fate, and one can see Nepalese striking their forehead, the place where the Almighty supposedly inscribes one's fate, with the palm of their hand in order to emphasise this. The belief is so strong that not only do almost all newspapers and magazines have their astrology columns (daily, weekly, even annually), but these columns remain extremely popular, with even the educated perusing them with the utmost seriousness.

The state of affairs prevailing in the Nepalese society can perhaps be gauged from a practice of the nineteenth century. Given that capital punishment was the norm at the time, those to be executed even had to bribe the executioners to make sure they had a clean cut, to make sure that the executions were carried out cleanly and with minimum pain to the executed. As the executioners did not have properly equipped weapons, sometimes those who were to be executed brought the weapons themselves. The executions were public affairs, and the spectators applauded after the deed had been performed. The spectators had no consideration for and were utterly indifferent towards the executed person's feelings, and expressed irritation at the delay as the executioners sharpened their weapons or searched for appropriate weapons (Oldfield 1981: 238-243). The "physical culture" prevalent in the Nepalese society can be seen from the use of words and phrases by parents even while berating their errant children (I will break your head, I will break your leg or even I will kill you!).

Modernity continues to exert considerable influence in our times, epistemologically as well as morally, and we, one way or the other, continue to walk in its light. Maybe there will be societies in the future that can do without modernity and all its achievements, including science and technology. After all, there have been societies in the past that have existed without science and, although it is difficult for us at present to conceive of such a thing, there may well be societies that will do so in the future as well. Nevertheless, to us as we exist today, modernity, despite the attacks upon it, remains a powerful "paradigm."

And, given that we are forced by circumstances to "act" within the time and place we happen to live in, the shirking of such a responsibility is not merely the act of a renunciate. It is also practically impossible. In this context, there have to be norms to guide our actions. And, while talking about norms and values, it might be worth stressing here that although time may be a road as well as a room, morality nonetheless should be—is?—always a "room." This can be illustrated with an example from our own history. Nepalese nationalist historians have traditionally put King Prithvi Narayan Shah on a pedestal, conferring upon him the title of "the Great," as one who "unified" the country. Today, however, with the "multinational" aspirations of the various groups in the Nepalese society, Prithvi Narayan Shah has come to be seen as a "bloody conqueror" and an "oppressor." In this regard, there have been comments about judging Prithvi Narayan by twentieth century human rights standards. But, on the other hand, there is also the danger of justifying even the caste system, untouchability or the mistreatment of women. Even more importantly, not thinking of morality as a room means that humans can become expendable "pawns" in the implacable march of progress and history. They can be sacrificed in the name of an abstract species, in the name of an abstract ideal, etc.

Therefore, along with much needed humility, there have to be certain norms and values to guide us. This includes a "minimalist universalism" that is mindful of basic decency and civility but is also equally mindful of the homogeneity that it can lead to. The attempt towards standardisation, and consequently homogenisation, is so strong that this has to be emphasised here.

Some Commonalities and Shared Values?

As we seek for norms and values to guide us to act within the time and place that we have to act, what can be those norms and values? Along with humility and respect for diversity, there are values like tolerance for others and their way of life that are important in an interconnected world. And—another important question in this regard—what can be the political system that can best protect and promote these values? While choosing an appropriate political system, I am aware that I can select only within the "paradigm" that I live in. And, unlike Francis Fukuyama although I do not claim it as the "final" form of government, I nevertheless do not see an alternative to the democratic system in the present world. Given this, should I also say that this democracy should go beyond the "minimalist" version and be liberal, i.e. it should hold certain individual rights as sacrosanct? Although there is "we-feeling" among groups like the indigenous nationalities, there is also diversity within the indigenous nationality groups. This diversity is "ideological" as well as related to the way the groups themselves came to be formed over time. Although some indigenous nationality intellectuals have claimed common ancestry of several indigenous nationality groups—according to this "story," the ten sons of a single father separated and later developed as various indigenous nationality groups (Yakharai 1996: 210)—anthropological evidence indicates otherwise. It is rather the disparate clans within a group that, through inter-marriage for instance, have come over time to form the currently existing groups (see, for instance, Subba 1999 and de Sales 2003).

The very process of group formation is a homogenising process by itself, as I have pointed out in Chapter Five. Nation building is inherently assimilationistic, and given the "multinational" nature of the Nepalese state, various groups have begun to conceive of themselves as nations. Given today's "paradigm" of nationalism, this, as I have argued previously, is not unjustified. (Though there are obviously contradictions vis-à-vis the process. An obvious one is the recruitment of Nepalese youths, especially Nepalese indigenous nationality youths, in Indian and British armies. Neither the "nationalist" Nepalese state nor the indigenous nationalities have till today unequivocally called for an end to this practice. Indeed, the status of "mercenary soldiers" is even occasionally seen as a matter of pride, including by the respective indigenous nationality groups themselves.)

As "nations," there are particularly two types of relationships to be taken into account. One is the relationship between nations, the inter-, while the other is the relationship within a nation, the intra-. The relationship between nations can take the form of conflicts, even war, while the relationship within a nation can lead to the suppressing of differing voices, as well as to conflicts and even occasionally war. Given that intra-group diversity is an inherent reality of all groups, the need for tolerance and respect for this diversity cannot be over-emphasised. This, in effect, means the acceptance of liberal principles, at least in some part if not in totality. The Nepalese society, one could say, is hardly a liberal society. One can see this not only in the intolerance for differing views and opinions, including political views and opinions, but also in social attitudes in general. The Nepal Police, for instance, carried out an 'operation' against youths with long hair and youths wearing earrings, tight jeans and fancy boots.

The bringing forth of laws, acts and programmes for the suppressing of differing and divergent views, opinions and attitudes, in the name of group interest, welfare, etc., can be a "slippery slope." When a communist party like the Unified Communist Party of Nepal (Maoist) says that it will not allow political parties aligned to feudalistic and imperialistic interests to operate under the new constitution, it not unnaturally raises apprehension among the other political forces of the country. Apart from the difficulty of defining "feudalistic and imperialistic interests," the provision can easily become a pretext for the prohibiting and banning of rival political parties. It can, consequently, lead to political intolerance, tyranny and totalitarianism.

A common refrain heard among politicians, intellectuals as well as concerned citizens in the Nepalese society is the lack of a "system." As a society supposedly in transition from a traditional to a modern one, many of the problems of the Nepalese society are seen as stemming from the absence of the "system" as found in modern "developed" societies. This may have to do with the following of traffic rules, the behaviour of public servants in government offices, the functioning of democracy or even such seemingly trivial issue as standing in queue properly. But, on the other hand, system can also become a straitjacket, stifling creativity and innovation. It can be a hindrance in adapting to the inevitably changing situations and circumstances we as human beings face in our everyday lives. Given this, can we say that the liberal provision of seeking for "external protection" for one's group but not imposing "internal restrictions" on the individual members of the group need not be regarded as inappropriate for groups like the indigenous nationalities?

If I have proposed the democratic system with appropriate liberal provisions as the suitable political system for the Nepalese indigenous nationalities, perhaps one could also make a similar claim vis-à-vis a secular state—another of the "ideological" pillars of a modernising Nepalese state. Although secularism as an ideal, an ideology, not to mention the secularisation of the society, may be—indeed, no doubt will be—opposed by religious groups, there nonetheless does not, given the multi-religious nature of the Nepalese society, appear to be an alternative to a religiously neutral secular state, as I have also argued elsewhere (Serchan 2007: 54). This is so even with regard to the remote mountainous region of the country with its overwhelming Buddhist population. Two issues come to mind in this context. One is that Buddhism, despite what its teachers and supporters would perhaps like to portray, is hardly a monolithic religion, with different sects and "schools." Another, and more important, is the fact that Buddhism in the Nepalese mountains is an "usurper" religion having imposed itself by "oppressing" pre-Buddhist traditions like *Bon*. A secular state, instead of a state associated with one particular religion, would mean that these alternative—even contrary—discourses will have better chance of expressing themselves in the public domain. (Nepalese Buddhists, given that the Buddha was born within the territories of present day Nepal and other such associations, have occasionally demanded that the country be declared a Buddhist state. The recent comment of a Buddhist monk-cum-Maoist Constituent Assembly member is in keeping with this. The Buddhist-Maoist in his comment not only justified the violence of the Maoists, but also stated that the new constitution to be made by the Constituent Assembly should in its preamble categorically mention Nepal as the country where the Buddha was born [*Kantipur* 2009: 9].)

Of course, Nepalese in their nationalist exuberance have claimed the Buddha as one of their own, i.e. as a Nepalese national. This primordial interpretation implies that there was during Buddha's time a 'Nepal' and 'Nepalese' as we know it today. Modernity's project of constructing a "religion of humanity" might have failed, but its "episteme" nonetheless continues to have its uses, as I have already mentioned. Nepalese indigenous nationality groups, not to mention indigenous peoples around the world, have occasionally confused their issue with "race." Those who have attended international fora of indigenous peoples mention the participants raising the issues of indigenous peoples as if it has something to do with race. In Nepal, the ethnic assertiveness has found expression in the form of not only political parties/organisations like the 'Mongol National Organisation' and 'Mongolian Revenge Group,' but has also found expression in the form of a 'Miss Mongol' beauty pageant, in which girls from various indigenous nationality groups took part. The issues of indigenous peoples is not something to do with "race" but of "groups," which by themselves have come to be formed through "accidents" of history. Referring to the various national groups of Europe, political scientist Walker Connor has pointed out that there was no predictable reason why the Slavic "tribes" did not evolve into a single nation, rather than fragmenting into the some fifteen Slavic peoples asserting nationhood. Also, if the assimilation of the continental Saxons into the German nation should have been anticipated, then how are we to account for the survival of the equally Germanic Dutch, Fleming, Frisian and Luxembourger peoples? Given that the nation is a self-defined entity, popular opinion could at any stage come to feel that the nation had been realised. Thus, Little Russians, i.e. Ukrainians, though related to the Great Russians, came increasingly in the twentieth century to feel that that relationship was not sufficiently close so as to represent a national bond (Connor 1994: 214).

Modernity's emphasis on human reason to solve all the world's ills may have been misplaced, but there does not seem any reason that humans should, therefore, dispense with this particular "tool" they have been endowed with by nature if it can, even if to a small extent, foster understanding and enhance the human condition. The argument that reason can be—has been—misused does not appear reason enough for the wholesale debunking of reason. Although there are limits to human reason—especially with regard to the "good life," as I have already mentioned—it nonetheless has proven its usefulness in various other areas of human life. With regard to the good life, the modern remains just one among the many ways to live one's life. The attempt to impose one's way of life on others in the name of humanitarian intervention and the like can only be termed as "liberal imperialism" or "neo-colonialism." Liberal societies cannot make the mistake of illiberal societies and claim that all societies follow the liberal ethos, nor can those who espouse the values of multiculturalism demand that all societies be multicultural. There will be societies that are illiberal as well as mono-cultural. This is a fine line that has to be walked, and virtues like humility, tolerance and understanding can be our guiding lights while we do so.

Although I have argued for some liberal values vis-à-vis groups like the Nepalese indigenous nationalities, there will obviously be those who will not concur with my viewpoint. As I have already mentioned, the Nepalese society is hardly a liberal society, and a political scientist has remarked upon the "centralising" tendency of the Nepalese (Lawoti 2005). This centralising tendency takes the form of intolerance for dissenting and opposing views. Although communist parties like the Maoists no doubt take the cake in this, as evinced in the colourful invective they use against those who do not agree with them (feudal, capitalist, reactionary, comprador, anti-national, imperialist, traitor, etc.), the other political parties of the country, too, are not blameless in this regard. Political parties, while undertaking their protest programmes like stopping of vehicular traffic, shut-downs, etc., have even gone to the extent of terrorising—this is not too strong a word—the public to enforce their writ. The burning of newspapers and books to express one's opposition to the views expressed therein is not uncommon among political parties and groups in the Nepalese society, including groups like the indigenous nationalities. On the other hand, anti-establishment protests against the Nepalese state in the post-1990 democratic dispensation have even taken the form of burning of the constitution and the "national" flag. There appear to be two things to be taken into consideration in this regard. One is that the state has tremendous powers to control and manipulate opinion and subvert opposition voices. This is true of not only an autocratic political system like the Panchayat of yore, which could imprison opposition leaders without trial for years, but also of the present democratic system. Given this, the state can afford to be tolerant and "magnanimous" with regard to the voices of oppressed and marginalised groups. As far as the oppressed and marginalised groups are concerned, one can understand their sensitivity vis-à-vis criticism. But criticism also allows one to learn from one's errors and mistakes, and the ability to be self-critical is not necessarily a bad thing. One could however say, in the present context, that those who offer their criticisms do so through reasoned argument. The satirising of oppressed and marginalised groups in novels or lampooning them in cartoons can only inflame the sentiments of the groups concerned. Maybe some day in the future these groups will be able to laugh at themselves, but in the present context one has to be understanding of their "touchiness." These groups, with the increase in self-confidence, will also come to realise that one can have multiple and complementary identities. As K. Anthony Appiah puts it,

> In policing this imperialism of identity—an imperialism as visible in racial identities as anywhere else—it is crucial to remember always that we are not simply black or white or yellow or brown, gay or straight or bisexual, Jewish, Christian, Moslem, Buddhist or Confucian, but we are also brothers and sisters; parents and children; liberals, conservatives and leftists; teachers and lawyers and auto-makers and gardeners; fans of the Padres and the Bruins; amateurs of grunge rock and lovers of Wagner; movie buffs; MTV-holics, mystery-readers; surfers and singers; poets and pet-lovers; students and teachers; friends and lovers. Racial identity can be the basis of resistance to racism—and though we have made great progress, we have further still to go—let us not let our racial identities subject us to new tyrannies (quoted in United Nations Development Programme 2004: 18).

As humans, we can—and have—multiple identities. And these identities need not be in conflict with one another. Indeed, they can be complementary of one another. Marginalised and oppressed groups like the indigenous nationalities have every right to protect and promote their language, culture and way of life. They can do this even as "nations" or "national" groups. Modernity's homogenising universalism would have the entire world made in its own image, little "Europes" and "Americas" around the world, so to say. But this, as I have argued, is wrong and fallacious thinking. One can argue for some basic decency and civility arising from our common humanity, certain moral values we all aspire towards because of our shared human-*ness*. Likewise, one could perhaps also claim for some common and shared "episteme." But all this, we have to remember, is just one step away from uniformity and homogeneity. It is not only the "wonders" of science but also "ideologies" like nationalism, democracy, development, etc. that continue to hold sway in the present world, and it is difficult, if not impossible, to "escape" from them, as this book is also testimony to. In the context of the homogenisation that these ideologies can so easily lead to, the affirmation of cultural pluralism (multiculturalism as an ideology!) becomes an urgent necessity. Different cultures can coexist with each other knowing that pride in one's own culture and way of life does not preclude respect and consideration for other cultures and ways of life. Just as one builds one's house for shelter knowing that there is an entire world beyond one's house, different cultures can live side by side knowing that there are other cultures and ways of life in existence as well. Also, despite our cultural differences, in a world that is interconnected, there are no strangers/outsiders and we, in spite of our differences, remain bound by the thread of our common humanity. For all those who are respectful of the world's diversity and plurality, it is an accepted, even cherished, principle that they remain tolerant and respectful of other cultures and ways of life, even of those cultures and ways of life that do not share their values of tolerance and diversity.

8

Conclusion

As we conclude this book, the first thing we may well admit is that modernity, for good or bad, represents a fundamental break from the past. It is "epochal" in the way that the onset of agriculture or the growth of the "world religions" was during the course of human history. And, like those history changing events, modernity also aspires towards the universal. That it does so, however, raises issues of considerable import, given that it is destructive of the world's diversity. Today, at the beginning of the twenty-first century, the thesis that the entire world conform to the West and attempt to be modern no longer remains valid. The world is "postmodern," as non-Western societies become self-confident and assertive vis-à-vis their own cultures and ways of life.

Nonetheless, modernity continues to cast its considerable shadow on our world. The "paradigm" of modernity and its ideologies continue to, if not dominate, influence the discourse of our times to a considerable extent. As an "epochal" event it is not surprising that modernity has "epistemic" as well as "moral" implications. Modernity's achievements thus remain not insignificant, despite all its excesses. But the claim that modernity be universal invites its own paradox. To be universal is to be one, in other words it is to negate the reality of a multicultural world. Even if the fruits of modernity could somehow be distributed equitably across all societies and peoples—which they have not been, as we have seen, and modernity remains fundamentally exclusionary and marginalising—the claim to 'oneness,' to universality and homogeneity is flawed, wrong. Modernity had ambitions to relieve humanity of all its ills, but instead went on to create its own "iron prison" of reason and bureaucracy. Given modernity's excesses, it is no longer "fashionable" today to believe in its vision of untramelled progress and development. This "progress" and "development," of course, led to iniquities, as the knowledge generated by modernity created its own haves and have-nots, those who could benefit from it and those who could not. As modernity has become global, peoples and societies around the world have been made to feel "inadequate" or "lacking" vis-à-vis this modernity. And modern knowledge has been used—or misused—to suppress, oppress and exploit peoples.

Although it will be foolhardy to dismiss all of the knowledge generated by modernity, including the theories of science, as ephemeral, as passing fads, there is much that remains more contentious. It is not only ideologies like liberalism, nationalism, secularism, etc., but also the very idea of progress and development that can be called into question in this regard. There can be alternative, even incompatible perspectives to these ideas and ideologies. Modernity is "unique"—not universal—and this uniqueness is its strength. Besides the "truths" of science, there are certain "values" that modernity has bequeathed us. These include the "negative freedoms," i.e. that individuals cannot be persecuted for their views or beliefs, that they cannot be physically abused or tortured or that they cannot be held in detention or imprisoned without the due process of law. And although modernity's belief in progress and development is just that—a belief—the idea that humans can better their condition through their own efforts can be contrasted with the fatalistic attitude of many traditional societies.

Modernity's influence, of course, is associated with the West's, i.e. the kernel of modernity own ascendancy over the rest of the world. Given this, modernity, for non-Western peoples, has often taken on a hegemonic form. But even if this were not so, the argument that the development trajectory to be followed by non-Western societies is the one already undergone by the West is fallacious. Modernity, in spite of its achievements, has no claim to universality. This includes even such uniquely modern achievement as science and all the epistemological advances that accompany it. There have been societies in the past that have existed without science, and there may well be societies in the future that could exist without it. Apart from the difficulty of constructing an independent rational justification for morality, it is, after all, not "will to knowledge" that drives human societies but rather the "will to power." Modernity, though it is a break from the past, thus remains only one among the many ways to live the "good" life.

Given this, the attacks that modernity is facing today cannot be considered as unexpected. The numerous "posts," as well as talk of the "end of ideology," point to something deeper, i.e. the malaise of modernity. The world today is "multicultural," with groups and peoples affirming their own identities. The world today is also more interconnected, "globalised." And as ıt has become so, it is in a way not surprising that groups and peoples have become more concerned vis-à-vis their own cultures and ways of life. There is apprehension that they will be forced, with the increasing globalisation, to assimilate into the so-called global culture, global civilisation, etc. In keeping with the paradox of universalisation, groups and peoples around the world are asserting the right to maintain and give continuity to their own cultures and ways of life in the face of globalisation.

Thus, the world is plural, multicultural, as well as being "globalised." No longer can the West assert unchallenged hegemony over the rest of the world. The diverse perspectives of groups and peoples around the world will come into play with regard to any issue. There is, in this context, the need for respecting the world's diversity as well as the necessity, in an increasingly interconnected world, of seeking amidst this diversity for some common and shared values of decency and civility that make worthwhile interaction among groups and peoples possible. And as we do so, it is not only the West and the modernity it engendered but the entire heritage of humanity from the past to the present that can be the guiding lights in our endeavours.

References

Abrams, M.H. 1988. "The deconstructive angel." In David Lodge, ed., *Modern Criticism and Theory: A Reader*. London and New York: Longman.

Ali, Tariq. 2003. *The Clash of Fundamentalisms: Crusades, Jihads and Modernity*. New Delhi: Rupa & Co.

Amin, Samir. 1997. *Capitalism in the Age of Globalization*. Delhi: Madhyam Books.

Anaya, S. James. 1996. *Indigenous Peoples in International Law*. New York: Oxford University Press.

Asimov, Isaac. 1960. *The Naked Sun*. St Albans, Herts AL22NF: Panther Books Ltd.

Beetham, David. 1993. "Liberal Democracy and The Limits of Democratization." In David Held, ed., *Prospects for Democracy: North, South, East, West*. Stanford: Stanford University Press.

Bhattachan, Krishna B. 1996. "Globalization and Its Impact on Nepalese Society and Culture." In *Impact of Globalization in Nepal*. Kathmandu: Nepal Foundation for Advanced Studies (NEFAS) and Friedrich-Ebert-Stiftung (FES), Nepal.

Bhattarai, Baburam. 2003. "The Political Economy of the People's War." In Arjun Karki and David Seddon, eds., *The People's War in Nepal: Left Perspectives*. Delhi: Adroit Publishers.

Bista, Dor Bahadur. 1991. *Fatalism and Development: Nepal's Struggle for Modernization*. Calcutta: Orient Longman Limited.

Blaikie, Piers, John Cameron and David Seddon. 1980. *Nepal in Crisis: Growth and Stagnation at the Periphery*. Delhi: Oxford University Press.

Camilleri, Joseph A. and Jim Falk. 1992. *The End of Sovereignty? The Politics of a Shrinking and Fragmenting World*. Hants, England: Edward Elgar Publishing Limited.

Caplan, Lionel. 1975. *Administration and Politics in a Nepalese Town*. London: Oxford University Press.

———. 2000. *Land and Social Change in East Nepal: A study of Hindu-tribal relations (Second Edition)*. Lalitpur, Nepal: Himal Books.

Chiriyankandath, James. 1997. "'Unity in Diversity'? Coalition Politics in India (with special reference to Kerala)." In *Democratization* (A Frank Cass Journal). Winter 1997, Volume 4, Number 4.

———. 1999. "Constitutional predilections." In *Multiculturalism: a symposium on democracy in culturally diverse societies*. http://www.india-seminar.com/1999/484.htm.

Connolly, William E. 2000. "The Liberal Image of the Nation." In Duncan Ivison, Paul Patton and Will Sanders, eds., *Political Theory and the Rights of Indigenous Peoples*. Cambridge: Cambridge University Press.

Connor, Walker. 1994. *Ethnonationalism: The Quest for Understanding*. Princeton, New Jersey: Princeton University Press.

CPN (Maoist). 2006. *Nepal Communist Party (Maobadi) ko Aitihasik Dastawejharu (Historical Documents of Communist Party of Nepal [Maoist])*. Biratnagar, Nepal: Prasabi Publications, CPN (Maoist), Mechi-Kosi Regional Bureau, Eastern Command.

de Sales, Anne. 2003. "The Kham Magar Country, Nepal Between Ethnic Claims and Maoism." In Deepak Thapa, ed., *Understanding the Maoist Movement of Nepal*. Kathmandu: Martin Chautari.

Deutscher, Isaac. 1984. "Marxism and Primitive Logic." In Tariq Ali, ed., *The Stalinist Legacy: Its Impact on Twentieth Century World Politics*. England: Penguin Books.

Devkota, Laxmi Prasad. 1963/64. *Laxmi Nibandha Sangraha (Collection of Essays by Devkota)*. Nepal: Nepali Bhasa Prakasini Samiti.

Dixit, Kanak Mani. 2003. "Insurgents and Innocents: The Nepali Army's Battle with The Maobadi." In Deepak Thapa, ed., *Understanding the Maoist Movement of Nepal*. Kathmandu: Martin Chautari.

———. 2006. "Nepalma Bideshi Sahayog: Hisab Dherai, Kam Sunya" (Foreign Aid in Nepal: Much Money, Nil Achievement). In Bhaskar Gautam, Jagannath Adhikari and Purna Basnet, eds., *Nepalma Garibiko Bahas*. Kathmandu: Martin Chautari.

Drucker, Peter F. 1994. *Post-Capitalist Society*. New York: HarperBusiness.

Durant, Will. 1954. *The Story of Civilization I: Our Oriental Heritage*. New York: Simon and Schuster.

Fisher, James F. 1987. ""Romanticism" and "Development" in Nepalese Anthropology." In *Occasional Papers in Sociology and Anthropology, Volume 1*. Kathmandu: Central Department of Sociology and Anthropology.

Friedman, Thomas L. 2007. "No, No, No, don't follow us." *The Kathmandu Post*, November 6.

Fukuyama, Francis. 1992. *The End of History and The Last Man*. London: Hamish Hamilton.

———. 1996. "The Primacy of Culture." In Larry Diamond and Marc F. Plattner, eds., *The Global Resurgence of Democracy*. Baltimore: The Johns Hopkins University Press.

Furer-Haimendorf, Christoph von. 1984. *The Sherpas Transformed*. New Delhi: Sterling Publishers Private Limited.

Gautam, Rajesh. 1989/90. *Nepalko Prajatantrik Andolanma Nepal Praja Parishadko Bhumika (The Role of Praja Parishad Party in Nepal's Democratic Development)*. Kathmandu.

Giddens, Anthony. 1990. *The Consequences of Modernity*. Cambridge: Polity Press.

Glazer, Nathan. 1998. "Individual Rights against Group Rights." In Gurpreet Mahajan, ed., *Democracy, Difference and Social Justice*. Delhi: Oxford University Press.

Gray, John. 1998. *Liberalism (Second Edition)*. Delhi: World View Publications.

Gupta, Dipankar. 1995. "Ethnicity, Religion, and National Politics in India." In Berch Berberoglu, ed., *The National Question: Nationalism, Ethnic Conflict, and Self-Determination in the 20th Century*. Philadelphia: Temple University Press.

———. 1998. "Recasting Reservations in the Language of Rights." In Gurpreet Mahajan, ed., *Democracy, Difference and Social Justice*. Delhi: Oxford University Press.

Gurung, Harka. 2001. *Nepalko Artha-Rajniti: Ganthan-Manthan (Political Economy of Nepal: Opinions and Analyses)*. Kathmandu: Deshbhakta Prajatantrik Manch.

Gyawali, Dipak. 2003. "Reflecting on Contemporary Nepali Angst." In Deepak Thapa, ed., *Understanding the Maoist Movement of Nepal*. Kathmandu: Martin Chautari.

———. 2006. "Hami Kin Garib?" (Why are we poor?). In Bhaskar Gautam, Jagannath Adhikari and Purna Basnet, eds., *Nepalma Garibiko Bahas*. Kathmandu: Martin Chautari.

Harvey, David. 1989. *The Condition of Postmodernity*. Cambridge MA & Oxford UK: Blackwell.

Himal Khabarpatrika. 2008. "Shahi Thathbath" (Royal way of life). December 16-30.

Hobsbawm, E.J. 1992. *The Age of Capital 1848-1875*. Calcutta: Rupa & Co.

Horgan, John. 1997. *The End of Science: Facing the Limits of Knowledge in the Twilight of the Scientific Age*. New York: Broadway Books.

Holmberg, David H. 1996. *Order in Paradox: Myth, Ritual, and Exchange Among Nepal's Tamang*. Delhi: Motilal Banarsidass Publishers.

Horsman, Mathew and Andrew Marshal. 1995. *After the Nation-State: Citizens, Tribalism and the New World Disorder*. London: HarperCollins Publishers.

Huntington, Samuel P. 1996. *The Clash of Civilizations and the Remaking of World Order*. New Delhi: Viking Penguin India.

INSEC. 1997. *Manavadhikar Barsha Pustak 1996 (Human Rights Yearbook 1996)*. Kathmandu: Informal Sector Service Centre.

Jackson, Dorothy. 2003. "Indigenous Advocacy in Central Africa." *Indigenous Affairs*, Issue 4.

Jensen, Marianne Wiben. 2003. "Editorial." *Indigenous Affairs*, Issue 4.

Kantipur. 2008. "Christian-Hindu Ek Thau" (Christians and Hindus in one place). October 4.

———. 2009. "Santika Prabakta" (Spokesperson for peace). April 30.

Kaviraj, S. 1996. "Planning and Panchayati Raj." In Adrian Leftwich, ed., *Democracy and Development*. Cambridge: Polity Press.

Keay, John. 2000. *India: A History*. London: HarperCollins Publishers.

Kennedy, Paul. 1994. *Preparing For The Twenty-First Century*. New Delhi: Indus – HarperCollins

Khilnani, Sunil. 1994. "India's Democratic Career." In John Dunn, ed., *Democracy: The Unfinished Journey 508 BC To AD 1993*. Oxford: Oxford University Press.

Kuhn, Thomas S. 1996. *The Structure of Scientific Revolutions (Third Edition)*. Chicago and London: The University of Chicago Press.

Kumar, Dhruba. 2000. "What Ails Democracy in Nepal?" In Dhruba Kumar, ed., *Domestic Conflict and Crises of Governability in Nepal*. Kathmandu: Centre for Nepal and Asian Studies.

Kymlicka, Will. 1995. *Multicultural Citizenship: A Liberal Theory of Minority Rights*. Oxford: Oxford University Press.

Lawoti, Mahendra. 2005. *Towards a Democratic Nepal: Inclusive Political Institutions for a Multicultural Society*. New Delhi: Sage Publications.

Lecomte-Tilouine, Marie. 2004. "Ethnic Demands within Maoism: Questions of Magar Territorial Autonomy, Nationality and Class." In Michael Hutt, ed., *Himalayan 'People's War': Nepal's Maoist Rebellion*. London: Hurst & Company.

Lenin, V.I. 1965. "The Constituent Assembly Elections and the Dictatorship of the Proletariat." In *Collected Works, Vol. 30*. Moscow: Progress Publishers.

Liechty, Mark. 2008. *Suitably Modern: Making Middle-Class Culture in Kathmandu*. Kathmandu: Martin Chautari.

Lyon, David. 2002. *Postmodernity (Second Edition)*. New Delhi: Viva Books Private Limited.

Mahajan, Gurpreet. 1998. "Introduction." In Gurpreet Mahajan, ed., *Democracy, Difference and Social Justice*. Delhi: Oxford University Press.

———. 1999. "Rethinking Multiculturalism." In *Multiculturalism: a symposium on democracy in culturally diverse societies*. http://www.india-seminar.com/1999/484.htm.

Michael, Bernardo A. 1999. "Statemaking and space on the margins of empire: Rethinking the Anglo-Gorkha war." In *Studies in Nepali History and Society*, Vol. 4, No. 2, December 1999. Kathmandu: Mandala Book Point.

Mills, C. Wright. 1962. *The Marxists*. New York: Dell Publishing Co., Inc.

Naraharinath, Yogi. 2000. "Biswas Nabhae Karyabhar Malai Dinu, Ma Garer Dekhaidinchhu" (Give me the responsibility if you do not believe me, I will do it and show the world). *Weekly Naya Current*, May 9.

NEFEN. 2003/04. *Bishwo Aadibasi Diwas, August 9, 2002: Pratibedan (International Day of the World's Indigenous Peoples, August 9, 2002: A Report)*. Kathmandu: Nepal Federation of Nationalities.

Nepal, Madhav Kumar. 2008. "Samyukta Sarkarka Jwalanta Samasya" (Burning problems of coalition government). *Kantipur*, October 26.

O'Donnel, Guillermo. 1998. "Horizontal Accountability in New Democracies." *Journal of Democracy*. Vol. 9, No. 3.

Oldfield, H. Ambrose. 1981. *Sketches from Nepal, Vol. 1*. Delhi: Cosmo Publications.

Panday, Bhim Bahadur. 1987/88. *Tyas Bhakhatko Nepal: Ranakalin Aakhiri Tin Dasak Part I (Nepal At That Time: The Last Three Decades of the Rana Rule Part I)*. Publisher: Author.

Panday, Devendra Raj. 2000. *Nepal's Failed Development: Reflections on the Mission and the Maladies*. Kathmandu: Nepal South Asia Centre.

Parekh, Bhikhu. 1993. "The Cultural Particularity of Liberal Democracy." In David Held, ed., *Prospects for Democracy: North, South, East, West*. Stanford: Stanford University Press.

———. 1999. "What is multiculturalism?" In *Multiculturalism: a symposium on democracy in culturally diverse societies*. http://www.india-seminar.com/1999/484.htm.

Pocock, J.G.A. 2000. "Waitangi as Mystery of State: Consequences of the Ascription of Federative Capacity to the Maori." In Duncan Ivison, Paul Patton and Will Sanders, eds., *Political Theory and the Rights of Indigenous Peoples.* Cambridge: Cambridge University Press.

Poffenberger, Mark. 1980. *Patterns of Change in the Nepal Himalaya*. Delhi: The Macmillan Company of India Limited.

Riley, Jonathon. 2002. "Defending Cultural Pluralism Within Liberal Limits." *Political Theory*, Vol. 30, No. 1.

Rose, Leo E. 1977. "King Mahendra's China Policy in Nepal." In S.D. Muni, ed., *An Assertive Monarchy*. New Delhi: Chetana Publications.

Rosenberg, Nathan and L.E. Birdzell, Jr. 1987. *How the West Grew Rich: The Economic Transformation of The Industrial World.* Bombay: Popular Prakashan.

Said, Edward W. 1995. *Orientalism: Western Conceptions of the Orient*. New York: Penguin Books.

Sakwa, Richard. 2002. *Postcommunism*. New Delhi: Viva Books Private Limited.

Sangari, Kumkum. 1999. "Which diversity?" In *Multiculturalism: a symposium on democracy in culturally diverse societies*. http://www.india-seminar.com/1999/484.htm.

Schumpeter, Joseph A. 1954. *Capitalism, Socialism and Democracy (Fourth Edition)*. London: Unwin University Books.

Seddon, David, Jagannath Adhikari and Ganesh Gurung. 2001. *The New Lahures: Foreign Employment and Remittance Economy of Nepal*. Kathmandu: Nepal Institute of Development Studies.

Serchan, Sanjaya. 2001. *Democracy, Pluralism and Change: An Inquiry in the Nepalese Context*. Kathmandu: Chhey Pahuppe.

———. 2007. *Remaking the Nepalese State*. Kathmandu: Sefavan Pi.

Shreshta, Badri Prasad. 2002. *Yojana, Budget ra Bikas: Barta-Antarbarta (Planning, Budget and Development: Talks-Interviews)*. Lalitpur, Nepal: Institute for Sustainable Development.

Smith, Mark J. 2002. *Culture: Reinventing the Social Sciences*. New Delhi: Viva Books Private Limited.

Srinivas, M.N. 1966. *Social Change in Modern India*. Berkeley: University of California Press.

Srivastava, S.K. 1999. "Culture Dynamics Among the Rana Tharus: The Past in the Present." In Harald O. Skar, ed., *Nepal: Tharu and Tarai Neighbours*. Kathmandu: EMR.

Stiller, Ludwig F., S.J. 1989. "Modern Nepal." In Kamal P. Malla, ed., *Nepal: Perspectives on Continuity and Change*. Kirtipur, Nepal: Centre for Nepal and Asian Studies.

Subba, T.B. 1999. *Politics of Culture*. Hyderabad: Orient Longman.

Subedi, Jhalak. 2004. "Godavariko Bhashan ra Comrade Powell" (Speech at Godavari and Comrade Powell). *Jana Aastha*, March 31.

Tamang, Seira. 2002. "The politics of 'developing Nepali women'." In Kanak Mani Dixit and Shastri Ramchandaran, eds., *State of Nepal*. Lalitpur, Nepal: Himal Books.

Taylor, Charles. 1994. *Multiculturalism: Examining the Politics of Recognition*. Princeton, New Jersey: Princeton University Press.

Taylor, Marc C. 2004. "The real meaning of deconstruction." *The Kathmandu Post*, October 16.

Tegegn, Melakou. 2003. "The Marginalization of Pastoral Communities in Ethiopia." *Indigenous Affairs*, Issue 4.

The Himalayan Times. 2009. "Nepal likely to face severe penalty." November 2.

Toffler, Alvin. 1981. *The Third Wave*. Toronto and New York: Bantam Books.

UNDP. 2002. *Nepal Human Development Report 2001: Poverty Reduction and Governance*. Kathmandu: United Nations Development Programme.

United Nations Development Programme. 2004. *Human Development Report: Cultural Liberty in Today's Diverse World*. New Delhi: Oxford University Press.

Walker, Graham. 1997. "The Idea of Nonliberal Constitutionalism." In Ian Shapiro and Will Kymlicka, eds., *Ethnicity and Group Rights*. New York and London: New York University Press.

Walzer, Michael. 1995. "Introduction." In Michael Walzer, ed., *Toward a Global Civil Society*. Providence and Oxford: Berghahn Books.

Yakharai, Durgahang. 1996. *Brahmanbad Biruddha Janajati+Utpidit Barg (Nationalities+Oppressed Classes Against Brahmanism)*.